Contents

List of resources	3
Introduction	4
How to use the CD-ROM	5

Mountain environments — PAGE 7

Notes on the CD-ROM resources	8
Notes on the photocopiable pages	20
Photocopiable pages	22

Coasts — PAGE 26

Notes on the CD-ROM resources	27
Notes on the photocopiable pages	40
Photocopiable pages	41

Rivers — PAGE 45

Notes on the CD-ROM resources	46
Notes on the photocopiable pages	58
Photocopiable pages	60

A contrasting UK locality: Parkgate — PAGE 64

Notes on the CD-ROM resources	65
Notes on the photocopiable pages	75
Photocopiable pages	77

Licence

IMPORTANT – PERMITTED USE AND WARNINGS – READ CAREFULLY BEFORE USING

Copyright in the software contained in this CD-ROM and in its accompanying material belongs to Scholastic Limited. All rights reserved. © Scholastic Ltd, 2005.

The material contained on this CD-ROM may only be used in the context for which it was intended in Ready Resources. School site use is permitted only within the school of the purchaser of the book and CD-ROM. Permission to download images is given for purchasers only and not for borrowers from any lending service. Any further use of the material contravenes Scholastic Ltd's copyright and that of other rights holders.

Save for these purposes, or as expressly authorised in the accompanying materials, the software may not be copied, reproduced, used, sold, licensed, transferred, exchanged, hired, or exported in whole or in part or in any manner or form without the prior written consent of Scholastic Ltd. Any such unauthorised use or activities are prohibited and may give rise to civil liabilities and criminal prosecutions.

This CD-ROM has been tested for viruses at all stages of its production. However, we recommend that you run virus-checking software on your computer systems at all times. Scholastic Ltd cannot accept any responsibility for any loss, disruption or damage to your data or your computer system that may occur as a result of using either the CD-ROM or the data held on it.

IF YOU ACCEPT THE ABOVE CONDITIONS YOU MAY PROCEED TO USE THIS CD-ROM

Text © Elaine Jackson
© 2005 Scholastic Ltd

Published by Scholastic Ltd, Villiers House,
Clarendon Avenue, Leamington Spa,
Warwickshire CV32 5PR

Printed by Bell & Bain Ltd, Glasgow

3 4 5 6 7 8 9 0   7 8 9 0 1 2 3 4

British Library Cataloguing-in-Publication Data
A catalogue record for this book is available from
the British Library.

ISBN 0-439-96489-X
ISBN 978-0439-96489-0

Visit our website at
www.scholastic.co.uk

CD developed in association with
Footmark Media Ltd

Author
Elaine Jackson

Editor
Christine Harvey

Project Editor
Wendy Tse

Assistant Editors
Aileen Lalor and Kim Vernon

Series Designer
Joy Monkhouse

Designer
Erik Ivens

Cover photographs
© DigitalVision/Getty Images

Acknowledgements

Extracts from the National Curriculum for England © Crown copyright material is reproduced with the permission of the Controller of HMSO and the Queen's Printer for Scotland. Extracts from Programmes of Study from The National Curriculum reproduced under the terms of HMSO Guidance Note 8. © Qualifications and Curriculum Authority.

Thank you to all the people of Parkgate who allowed us to use images of their premises.

Every effort has been made to trace copyright holders and the publishers apologise for any omissions.

Due to the nature of the web, the publisher cannot guarantee the content or links of any of the websites referred to. It is the responsibility of the reader to assess the suitability of websites.

The rights of Elaine Jackson to be identified as the author of this work have been asserted by her in accordance with the Copyright, Designs and Patents Act 1988.

All rights reserved. This book is sold subject to the condition that it shall not, by way of trade or otherwise, be lent, hired out or otherwise circulated without the publisher's prior consent in any form of binding or cover other than that in which it is published and without a similar condition, including this condition, being imposed upon the subsequent purchaser.
   No part of this publication may be reproduced, stored in a retrieval system, or transmitted, in any form or by any means, electronic, mechanical, photocopying, recording or otherwise, without the prior permission of the publisher. This book remains copyright, although permission is granted to copy pages where indicated for classroom distribution and use only in the school which has purchased the book and in accordance with the CLA licensing agreement. Photocopying permission is given only for purchasers and not for borrowers of books from any lending service.

Made with Macromedia is a
trademark of Macromedia, Inc.
Director ®
Copyright © 1984-2000
Macromedia, Inc.

Minimum Specifications:
PC: Windows 98 SE or higher
Processor: Pentium 2 (or equivalent) 400 MHz
RAM: 128 Mb
CD-ROM drive: 48x (52x preferred)

MAC: OS 9.2 (OSX preferred)
Processor: G3 400 MHz
RAM: 128 Mb
CD-ROM drive: 48x (52x preferred)

List of resources on the CD-ROM

The page numbers refer to the teacher's notes provided in this book.

Mountain environments

Mountains around the world	8
Mount Aconcagua	8
Videos: Volcanic eruption at Réunion, Volcanic eruption at Mount Etna, Audio: Volcanic eruption	9
Climbing Everest	10
Austrian Tyrol	11
The Himalayas	12
Avalanche, Audio: Avalanche	12
Aftermath of avalanche	13
The largest glacier in Europe	14
Map of France, Diagram of Châtel	15
Châtel in winter, Skiing at Châtel	16
Châtel in summer	16
The Lake District in the United Kingdom	17
OS map of the Lake District	18
Grasmere	18
Farmhouse near Grasmere	19
Sarah Nelson's gingerbread shop	20

Coasts

Map of the Purbeck coast	27
Hengistbury Head	27
Cove	28
Coastal arches	28
Stacks and stumps	29
Bars and spits	29
Barton-on-Sea cliff face, Warning sign	30
Collapse of a cliff	31
Groynes	31
A revetment	32
Dykes	32
Bournemouth: busy seaside, Bournemouth: sandy beach	33
Video: Aerial beach scene	34
Video: Windsurfing	34
Ferry terminal at Dover	34
Fleetwood fishing port	35
Pleasure boats in Poole Harbour	36
Offshore wind farm	36
Offshore oil platform	37
Litter on beaches	37
Sea Empress clean-up operation	38
Rescue operation of oiled birds	39

Rivers

Rivers around the world	46
Rivers in Europe	46
Rivers in the British Isles	47
The water cycle	47
Source of the River Ganges	47
Victoria Falls	48
Buttermere Valley	49
Confluence of the Rio Negro and the River Amazon	49
Meanders on the River Cuckmere	50
Delta of the River Nile	50
Transporting goods on the River Rhine	51
Ferry at Dartmouth	52
Canoeing on the River Dee	52
Three Gorges Dam on the River Yangtze	53
Women washing on the River Ganges, Pilgrims on the River Ganges	53
Chemical pollution	54
Rubbish on rivers	55
Flooding at Bewdley 1998	55
Flood barriers at Bewdley 2004	56
Floods in Mozambique 2000	57
Floods in Prague 2002	58

A contrasting UK locality: Parkgate

World map	65
Parkgate in the British Isles	65
Wirral peninsula map	66
OS map of Parkgate	66
The River Dee	67
Parkgate promenade 1950	68
Parkgate promenade 2004	68
At the seaside 1890	69
Watching from the slip 1890s	69
Loading cockles and mussels 1940s	69
Shrimp and cockle shop 2004	70
Parkgate Station 1906	70
The Wirral Way	70
Boat House restaurant	71
Birdwatching	72
Watch Tower House	72
Dover Cottage	72
New houses 1998	73
New houses 2003	73
Ice cream shop, The Marsh Cat restaurant, The Red Lion, Old Quay Inn	74
Parkgate Primary School	74
Mostyn House Independent School	75
Garden centre	75
Pony sanctuary	75

INTRODUCTION

This book and CD-ROM support the teaching and learning set out in the QCA Scheme of Work for geography in Years 1 and 2. The CD provides a large bank of resources – both visual and aural. The book provides teachers' notes, which offer background information, ideas for discussion and activities to accompany the CD resources. There are also photocopiable pages to support the teaching. All have been specifically chosen to meet the requirements for resources listed in the QCA units for Years 1 and 2. Some additional resources and ideas have also been included to enable teachers to develop and broaden these areas of study if they wish. These include activity sheets to help children clarify their thinking or to record what they find out.

The resources and activities are not intended to provide a structure for teaching in themselves, but are designed to provide a basis for discussion and activities that focus on the knowledge, skills and understanding required by the National Curriculum for geography. The children are encouraged to develop such key skills as observing, questioning, describing, sorting and sequencing.

Graphicacy is one of the key skills in geography and it covers all forms of pictorial communication of spatial information: ground-level photographs, oblique and vertical aerial photographs, diagrams, signs and symbols, and maps of all sorts – from pictorial to Ordnance Survey. Maps and their conventional use of plan view are important in geography, but children see their world from eye-level. There is a large conceptual leap between eye-level and plan (aerial) view so children can be helped to make sense of, and understand, the relationship between horizontal and vertical viewpoints by the use of intermediate perspectives, that is, views taken from a range of oblique angles.

Links with other subjects

Research skills
Independent enquiry and the development of research skills are important in this book. The children are encouraged to use reference books and the internet to gather further information related to a topic. Work of this kind will help foster an independent, enquiring attitude on the part of the children, helping them to become more effective learners.

Literacy
There are a number of close links between the units covered in this book and work on literacy. The discussion activities contribute directly to the requirements for speaking and listening. There is considerable opportunity for the children to develop their independent writing skills as they write simple captions using the word cards. Images from the CD could be printed to stimulate independent writing, or to illustrate it.

Maths
Skills such as counting, measuring, matching, ordering and sequencing are essential to both geography and maths. Measuring skills are fostered when children calculate distances. The children are required to make calculations, for instance calculating the temperature loss depending on how high up a mountain a climber is.

Science
In discussing the water cycle, the children can link how the changing state and movements of water relate to the development of geographical features.

History
Children learn about the history of a settlement in the study of a local area, in this case Parkgate in Cheshire. Children are encouraged to think about how and why a settlement has changed, and how development can be influenced by geographical location.

ICT
Children are encouraged to use the internet whenever possible to search for more information on subjects they are studying.

HOW TO USE THE CD-ROM

Windows NT users
If you use Windows NT you may see the following error message: 'The procedure entry point Process32First could not be located in the dynamic link library KERNEL32.dll'. Click on **OK** and the CD will autorun with no further problems.

Setting up your computer for optimal use
On opening, the CD will alert you if changes are needed in order to operate the CD at its optimal use. There are three changes you may be advised to make:

Viewing resources at their maximum screen size
To see images at their maximum screen size, your screen display needs to be set to 800 x 600 pixels. In order to adjust your screen size you will need to **Quit** the program.

If using a PC, open the **Control Panel**. Select **Display** and then **Settings**. Adjust the **Desktop Area** to 800 x 600 pixels. Click on **OK** and then restart the program.

If using a Mac, from the **Apple** menu select **Control Panels** and then **Monitors** to adjust the screen size.

Adobe Acrobat Reader
To print high-quality versions of images and to view and print the photocopiable pages on the CD you need **Adobe Acrobat Reader** installed on your computer. If you do not have it installed already, a version is provided on the CD. To install this version **Quit** the 'Ready Resources' program.

If using a PC, right-click on the **Start** menu on your desktop and choose **Explore**. Click on the + sign to the left of the CD drive entitled 'Ready Resources' and open the folder called 'Acrobat Reader Installer'. Run the program in this folder to install **Adobe Acrobat Reader**.

If using a Mac, double-click on the 'Ready Resources' icon on the desktop and on the 'Acrobat Reader Installer' folder. Run the program contained in this folder to install **Adobe Acrobat Reader**.

PLEASE NOTE: If you do not have **Adobe Acrobat Reader** installed, you will not be able to print high-quality versions of images, or to view or print photocopiable pages (although these are provided in this book and can be photocopied).

It is recommended that certain images, such as maps and aerial views, are viewed and printed in **Adobe Acrobat Reader** as it will be easier to zoom in to focus on specific areas.

QuickTime
In order to view the videos and listen to the audio on this CD you will need to have **QuickTime version 5 or later** installed on your computer. If you do not have it installed already or have an older version of QuickTime, the latest version can be downloaded at http://www.apple.com/quicktime/download/win.html. If you choose to install this version, **Quit** the 'Ready Resources' program.

PLEASE NOTE: If you do not have **QuickTime** installed you will be unable to view the films.

Menu screen
- Click on the **Resource Gallery** of your choice to view the resources available under that topic.
- Click on **Complete Resource Gallery** to view all the resources available on the CD.
- Click on **Photocopiable Resources (PDF format)** to view a list of the photocopiables provided in this book.
- **Back**: click to return to the opening screen. Click **Continue** to move to the **Menu screen**.
- **Quit**: click to close the menu program and progress to the **Quit screen**. If you quit from the **Quit screen** you will exit the CD. If you do not quit you will return to the **Menu screen**.

Resource Galleries
- **Help**: click **Help** to find support on accessing and using images.
- **Back to menu**: click here to return to the **Menu screen**.
- **Quit**: click here to move to the **Quit screen** – see **Quit** above.

Viewing images
Small versions of each image are shown in the Resource Gallery. Click and drag the slider on the slide bar to scroll through the images in the Resource Gallery, or click on the arrows to move the images frame by frame. Roll the pointer over an image to see the caption.
▶ Click on an image to view the screen-sized version of it.
▶ To return to the Resource Gallery click on **Back to Resource Gallery**.

Viewing videos
Click on the video icon of your choice in the Resource Gallery. In order to view the videos on this CD, you will need to have **QuickTime** installed on your computer (see 'Setting up your computer for optimal use' above).

Once at the video screen, use the buttons on the bottom of the video screen to operate the video. The slide bar can be used for a fast forward and rewind. To return to the Resource Gallery click on **Back to Resource Gallery**.

Listening to sound recordings
Click on the required sound icon. Use the buttons or the slide bar to hear the sound. A transcript will be displayed on the viewing screen where appropriate. To return to the Resource Gallery, click on **Back to Resource Gallery**.

Printing
Click on the image to view it (see 'Viewing images' above). There are two print options:

Print using Acrobat enables you to print a high-quality version of an image. Choosing this option means that the image will open as a read-only page in **Adobe Acrobat** and in order to access these files you will need to have already installed **Adobe Acrobat Reader** on your computer (see 'Setting up your computer for optimal use' above). To print the selected resource, select **File** and then **Print**. Once you have printed the resource **minimise** or **close** the Adobe screen using – or **X** in the top right-hand corner of the screen. Return to the Resource Gallery by clicking on **Back to Resource Gallery**.

Simple print enables you to print a lower quality version of the image without the need to use **Adobe Acrobat Reader**. Select the image and click on the **Simple print** option. After printing, click on **Back to Resource Gallery**.

Slideshow presentation
If you would like to present a number of resources without having to return to the Resource Gallery and select a new image each time, you can compile a slideshow. Click on the + tabs at the top of each image in the Resource Gallery you would like to include in your presentation (pictures, sound and video can be included). It is important that you click on the images in the order in which you would like to view them (a number will appear on each tab to confirm the order). If you would like to change the order, click on **Clear slideshow** and begin again. Once you have selected your images – up to a maximum of 20 – click on **Play slideshow** and you will be presented with the first of your selected resources. To move to the next selection in your slideshow click on **Next slide**, to see a previous resource click on Previous slide. You can end your slideshow presentation at any time by clicking on **Resource Gallery**. Your slideshow selection will remain selected until you Clear slideshow or return to the **Menu screen**.

Viewing on an interactive whiteboard or data projector
Resources can be viewed directly from the CD. To make viewing easier for a whole class, use a large monitor, data projector or interactive whiteboard. For group, paired or individual work, the resources can be viewed from the computer screen.

Photocopiable resources (PDF format)
To view or print a photocopiable resource page, click on the required title in the list and the page will open as a read-only page in **Adobe Acrobat**. In order to access these files you will need to have already installed **Adobe Acrobat Reader** on your computer (see 'Setting up your computer for optimal use' above). To print the selected resource select **File** and then **Print**. Once you have printed the resource **minimise** or **close** the Adobe screen using – or **X** in the top right-hand corner of the screen. This will take you back to the list of PDF files. To return to the **Menu screen**, click on **Back**.

MOUNTAIN ENVIRONMENTS

Content and skills
The content in this chapter supports the activities in unit 15, 'The mountain environment', of the QCA Scheme of Work for geography at Key Stage 2. It supports the unit by providing some necessary resources for exploring ideas related to upland and mountainous environments, and how the climate and terrain affects people and their lives.

The content supplements and extends the unit by exploring different mountain environments throughout the world. The chapter begins by developing the children's understanding of the distribution of major mountain ranges throughout the world. Through the resources, children are encouraged to find out about the impact of climate on the weathering processes, the vegetation and how the land on the slopes is used. Mountain localities in different parts of the world are used as examples, so children can compare and contrast aspects of the physical features and life in those places. The impact of natural disasters on life (such as avalanches and volcanic eruptions) and tourism is also explored.

Châtel Tourist Office © Jean François Vuarand

Resources on the CD-ROM
The resources include maps, oblique aerial photographs, ground-level photographs, video footage and audio tracks. Through the use of these good quality secondary resources, alongside independent research using ICT and other resources, the children will develop a good understanding of mountain environments around the world. The resources reflect a balance of approach, so that an understanding of the physical processes and human development are explored side-by-side.

Photocopiable pages
The photocopiable resources within the book will enable children to understand the different features of mountain environments They are also provided in PDF format on the CD and can be printed out from there. They include:
▶ word cards on climate and terrain
▶ word cards to describe tourist activities in Alpine regions
▶ labelled diagrams that will give the children an understanding of how glaciers develop and erode on the landscape and of how avalanches are formed
▶ a labelling exercise to help the children develop an understanding of how mountaineers protect themselves from the adverse weather conditions in mountainous areas.

The teacher's notes that accompany the photocopiable pages include suggestions for developing discussion and using them as whole-class, group or individual activities.

Geographical skills
Skills developed by activities using the resources in this chapter include map reading and interpretation, identification of key features within visual images and the development of the relevant geographical vocabulary, and describing different mountain environments. Geographical enquiry is promoted and children are encouraged to ask geographical questions, collect and analyse the evidence, and draw conclusions. The children are encouraged to identify and explain the different views people hold about geographical issues, such as tourism in mountainous areas. Knowledge and understanding of places is developed, as children locate mountainous areas, describe where the places are, why they are like they are, and how and why places change over time. Children will also learn to understand how people can improve and manage mountainous environments sustainably or damage the environment.

NOTES ON THE CD-ROM RESOURCES

Mountains around the world

The map shows the major mountain ranges and peaks of the world (one on each continent, except Antarctica). Mountains were formed many years ago by slow but gigantic movements of the earth's surface (crust). Sometimes parts of the crust have pushed against each other and folded and buckled, while other parts have pulled apart causing it to break into huge blocks. In both cases, great areas of land are lifted upwards to form mountains.

Mountains make up about one-fifth of the world's landscape, and provide homes to at least one-tenth of the world's people. Mountains are found on all continents and there are even mountains under the surface of the sea! Most mountains are found in long chains called 'mountain ranges'. The highest mountain range is the Himalayas in Asia. Mountains such as Mount Kenya (Africa) and Mount Fuji (Japan) stand alone.

Discussing the map
▶ Explain to the children that this is a physical map of the world, a relief map, and shows the continents, major mountain ranges and peaks.
▶ Tell the children that relief maps use shading to show upland areas, while topographical maps show all the natural features of the area (including lakes and rivers) and use contour lines.
▶ Explain that areas of mountain are identified by shading on the map and peaks by a triangle symbol and their name and spot height.
▶ Explain that a group of mountains is called a 'range' and mountain ranges have names to identify them. Allow the children time to explore the map and to locate the main mountain ranges.

Activities
▶ In small groups, ask the children to discuss the differences between a hill and a mountain. Take feedback from the groups, and discuss the ideas and definitions. There is not a world-agreed definition of a mountain, so ask the children, using different dictionaries, to find definitions for the word and then to produce a definition agreed by their group. Share and discuss the definitions as a whole class.
▶ Ask the children to list the seven continents of the world, and to name a mountain range in each along with the highest mountain. Then ask the children to place the mountains in order of height from the highest to the lowest.
▶ Give the children an outline map of the world showing the continents. Ask them to mark, shade and label the main mountain ranges and the continents. Then, using an atlas, ask them to mark on any solitary mountains, such as Mount Egmont (New Zealand) and Mount Fuji (Japan). They could create a key for their map.
▶ Give the children a copy of the map and ask them to mark which mountain ranges stretch from north to south and which ranges stretch from east to west.
▶ Ask the children, using reference books and the internet, to research a mountain range and then produce a fact file. Ask questions to prompt their thinking, such as How was it formed? What is the scenery like? What is the climate like? Who lives in the mountain range?
▶ Ask the children to find out about an upland area (hilly area) in or near to their local area. Ask them to produce some information text about this area.

Mount Aconcagua

The Andes are located in South America, and run generally parallel to the Pacific coast for more than 8000 km. They extend from Tierra del Fuego northward, across the equator, as the backbone of the entire continent. The Andes go through seven South American countries: Argentina, Chile, Bolivia, Peru, Colombia, Ecuador and Venezuela.

This photograph shows Aconcagua (6960m) in western Argentina, the highest mountain in the Western hemisphere. As you travel up a mountain, such as Aconcagua, the weather changes and the temperature falls at a rate of 2°C for every 300m you climb. If you climb high enough, you will eventually reach the snow line. Above this line it is so cold that snow

MOUNTAIN ENVIRONMENTS

covers the ground even in summer and this is why there is snow on the tops of very high mountains near the Equator. Glaciers, rivers of ice, are found above the snow line of many mountains. A glacier is a slow-moving river of ice (see the notes for 'The largest Glacier in Europe' on page 14 for further details).

Mountains are often covered in clouds. Mountains force the wind, carrying tiny droplets of water, to rise, forming clouds. Winds sometimes blow across the tops of mountains. As the droplets of water get bigger, they fall as rain or snow (precipitation). Often, rain or snow only falls on one side of a mountain, the windward side. The other side of the mountain, the leeward side, receives much less rain and snow, and is in the 'rain shadow'.

The sun affects the sides of mountains differently. Sometimes, one side of a mountain may be in sunshine for long periods while the other side may be in shadow. Valley bottoms are often colder than the lower slopes, because cold air is heavier and sinks into the valleys.

Mountains are constantly being worn away by a process called 'weathering'. The three main types of weathering are physical, chemical and biological:
▶ Physical: rainwater gets into tiny cracks in the rocks, and as it freezes and turns into ice it expands, pressing on the sides of the crack and weakening it until pieces break off. The constant changes in temperature in mountain areas make the rocks expand and shrink, so causing weaknesses and the rocks to break up.
▶ Chemical: rainwater is slightly acidic and this can slowly dissolve rock surfaces.
▶ Biological: the roots of plants force their way through gaps and cracks, forcing them to widen. Animals burrowing often cause fragments to break off, too.

Discussing the photograph
▶ Explain to the children that this photograph shows Aconcagua, the highest mountain in the Western hemisphere. Tell them that it is in the Andes mountain range.
▶ Explain where Aconcagua and the Andes are located (see above).
▶ Ask the children why they think there is snow and cloud at the top of mountains. Discuss with the children how climate changes as you go up a mountain.

Activities
▶ Ask the children to locate South America, the Andes, Aconcagua, Argentina, Chile, Bolivia, Peru, Colombia, Ecuador and Venezuela on a map.
▶ Tell the children the rate of temperature change for a mountain such as Aconcagua. Giving them the height of the mountain (see above), ask them to calculate how much the temperature would fall if they climbed from sea level to the top of Aconcagua.
▶ Ask the children to write a documentary presentation about mountains and climate and to show this to the class using PowerPoint. The children could use photographs from the Resource Gallery to illustrate their points.
▶ Ask the children to undertake further research on the process of mountain weathering. They could use CD-ROMs, reference books and the internet.

Videos: Volcanic eruption at Réunion, Volcanic eruption at Mount Etna, Audio: Volcanic eruption

A volcano is formed where magma (rock from the earth's interior) is made molten (or liquid) by high temperature, and erupts through the earth's surface. Volcanoes may be either dormant (having no activity) or active (having near constant expulsion and occasional eruptions) and are unpredictable. Around the world there are more than a thousand active volcanoes, which are constantly changing the shape of the land. They are all different. Some erupt fairly quietly, while others erupt with explosive violence. The kind of magma inside the volcano makes the difference between it being quiet or dramatically explosive, and the shape of the volcano depends on the material it exudes. Magma is forced upwards and flows out across the earth's surface as lava. Rising magma can heat the water in the rock and surrounding water features, and can cause explosive discharges of steam. If the magma is full of gas, the gas pressure inside the volcano can build up until it explodes violently, ejecting rocks, cinders, volcanic gas and volcanic ash.

The consistency of the lava determines the shape of the volcano, depending on how runny it is. If it is viscous, it flows slowly down slopes. These slopes are often steep, resulting in a tall volcano where the base does not cover a large area. Volcanoes such as Mount Fuji

MOUNTAIN ENVIRONMENTS

(Japan), Vesuvius (Italy), Mount Erebus (Antarctica) and Mount Rainier (north-western America) are tall conical mountains composed of both lava flows and ejected material.

If the lava is fluid and runs like water it can cover a large area quickly. The type of volcano formed has gradual slopes, is not very tall and can have a base covering hundreds of square kilometres. These type of volcanoes are often called shield volcanoes. Hawaii and Iceland are examples of places where volcanoes extrude huge quantities of lava that gradually build a wide mountain with a shield-like profile. The largest lava shield is Mauna Loa (Hawaii). It is 9144m high (it sits on the sea floor) and 121km in diameter.

Discussing the videos and sound

▶ Explain to the children that the 'Volcanic eruption at Réunion' video shows a volcanic eruption, where magma (red hot molten rock) is shooting into the air. The red-hot magma, known as lava when it reaches the earth's surface, starts to flow down the side of the volcano, destroying everything in its path.

▶ Explain where the island of Réunion is (in the Indian Ocean, east of Madagascar and south west of Mauritius).

▶ Discuss with the children the background to volcanoes, so they have an understanding of the difference the consistency of the lava makes to the type of explosion and the shape of the volcano that evolves (see above).

▶ Explain to the children that the 'Volcanic eruption at Mount Etna' video shows an explosive volcano, Mount Etna in Sicily. The video shows clouds of white-hot ash, red-hot shattered rock, gas and steam being blasted out from the volcano. These can be deadly. It was the exceptionally heavy fall of ash that killed people by the thousand in Pompeii, Italy. The gases given off include sulphuric acid and hydrogen sulphide, which are poisonous. Carbon dioxide is also released, causing people and animals to suffocate.

▶ Play the 'Volcanic eruption' audio file to the children. Ask them what they imagine is happening.

Activities

▶ Using reference books, ask the children to find six volcanoes around the world. Give them a blank outline map and ask them to mark the volcanoes on it.

▶ Let the children make a papier-mâché model of a volcano with a hole in the top. Demonstrate how to insert an upturned plastic bottle top into the hole. Fill this with baking powder and make a slight depression in the middle. Add a tablespoon of vinegar and watch what happens (the mixture will fizz and spill over the sides of the volcano. Repeat the activity several times adding a different powder to the baking powder (turmeric, paprika) each time to emphasise the layering effect.

▶ Demonstrate the cooling process of lava for the children. To do this, warm black treacle in a bowl over a pan of hot water. When the treacle is runny, ask a child to record the temperature and pour a tablespoonful onto an inclined slope. Ask another child to record how long the treacle takes to stop flowing, the distance it travels in a minute and the distance successive treacle 'lava' flows travel (each time starting with the treacle at a cooler temperature). Ask for suggestions about how to make this a fair test, and ask the children to record and discuss the results.

Climbing Everest

This photograph shows Mount Everest in the Himalayas. At 8850m (from sea level) it is the highest mountain in the world. However, measured from its base, 4931m below the sea surface, to its summit, 4169m above sea level, Mauna Loa in Hawaii beats Mount Everest by 252m. Mount Everest has many glaciers. Glaciers are permanently frozen snow and ice.

Mount Everest is named after a British military engineer called Sir George Everest. He was Surveyor General of India from 1829 to 1843 and during this time he surveyed the peak. He was the first person to record the location and height of Mount Everest, which at that time was called Peak XV. In May 1953, Sir Edmund Hillary and Tenzing Norgay became the first people in the world to climb to the top of Mount Everest.

When climbing Mount Everest, climbers have to carry oxygen in bottles with them, as the air is thin. As shown in the photograph, climbers need climbing boots, crampons, goggles and ice axes. (For further information, see 'The Himalayas' on page 12.)

MOUNTAIN ENVIRONMENTS

Discussing the photograph
▶ Explain that Mount Everest is the highest mountain in the world and facilitate a whole-class discussion about what the children already know about Mount Everest.
▶ Describe the climate on Mount Everest.
▶ Ask the children what is happening in the photograph. Discuss the climber and the equipment he needs to climb Mount Everest.
▶ Ask the children why they think some people want to climb Mount Everest. Ask them to give reasons why they would or wouldn't want to climb the mountain.

Activities
▶ Give the children a copy of the photograph and ask them to label all the physical features they can see (ice, snow, peak, slope, ridge, rock, glacier).
▶ Ask the children, using reference books, CD-ROMS and the internet, to find out about the Himalayas. Who lives there? What plants and animals live there? What impact do the Himalayas have on the lives of the people who live there?
▶ Challenge the children to use thought bubbles to describe how they would feel if they were the climber in the photograph.
▶ Using reference books, CD-ROMS and the internet, ask the children to find out about Sir Edmund Hillary and write a short biography of him.
▶ Give the children a copy of the 'Mountain climber' sheet on photocopiable page 25 to complete. Ask the children to find some of the equipment on the climber in the photograph.

Austrian Tyrol

The Alps is the collective name for one of the vast mountain systems of Europe, stretching over 965 kilometres. The Alps are the second highest mountain range in the world. They include several hundred peaks and glaciers, with Mont Blanc on the French-Italian border the highest at 4808m.

Austria is a landlocked country in central Europe. Austria's west and south are situated in the Alps, making it a well-known winter sports destination. The highest mountain in Austria is the Grossglockner at 3798m above sea level, followed by the Wildspitze at 3774m. In the Alps the climate depends more upon the height above sea level than anything else. Summers tend to be warm but wet, while snow lies deep during winter.

This photograph shows a village in the Austrian Tyrol, a region of outstanding beauty, where panoramic mountain scenery with snow-capped peaks tower above fast-flowing rivers and flower-filled green meadows. Picturesque villages of rustic wooden chalets are dotted over the landscape. The mountains have moulded Tyrolean life and there is a strong sense of Tyrolean identity. The high alpine meadows are used for grazing cattle and prize-winning cheeses are made in the mountains. The soil is too thin and the slopes too steep for other crops to be grown. The traditional dress of lederhosen and feathered hats is commonly seen, and the region has many colourful folklore and customs, including Schuhplatter dancing, brass bands and yodelling.

Above the pasture land is a zone of coniferous forest, passing into scrubland and bare rock the further up the mountain you travel. The snow line is reached, above which there are areas of perpetual snow and ice.

The Tyrol is a paradise for anyone who enjoys the great outdoors, offering excellent downhill and cross-country skiing in winter, and wonderful walking and hiking in summer.

Discussing the photograph
▶ Explain to the children that this photograph shows a fairly typical village in the Austrian Tyrol. Do the children know what the houses are called and what they are made of?
▶ What can the children see in the foreground of the photograph? (Cattle grazing.) Explain that the cows' milk is made into cheese. Tell the children that the soil in the area is too thin and the slopes are too steep for other crops to be grown.
▶ Can the children see how the vegetation changes the higher up the mountainside you look? Explain to them what levels of vegetation lie above the pasture land (see above).
▶ Explain that the photograph was taken in summer and discuss how this view would look very different in the winter months.

Activities

▶ Using atlases, ask the children to locate Austria, draw a sketch map of it and label the countries that surround it. Ask them to mark on the highest mountain in the country.
▶ In groups, ask the children to consider the mountain climate, and list what factors impact on the weather and vegetation.
▶ Ask the children, in groups, to make a collage to represent this mountain environment in either winter or summer.
▶ Ask the children to write a report on why a visit to this area might not be suitable for (a) small children or (b) disabled people.

The Himalayas

This is a photograph of the peaks of the high Himalayan mountains. The Himalayas is a mountain system in Asia, comprising three main ranges. They are relatively young fold mountains, formed about 38 million years ago. They stretch for 2500km from Pakistan in the west to China in the east. The largest area under snow outside the polar regions, 14 of the highest mountain peaks and some of the deepest valleys in the world are found here. The Indus, Ganges and Brahmaputra rivers all have their sources in the Himalayas.

High in the Himalayas the climate is cold and harsh. The land is permanently covered in snow and ice. The Himalayas protect the rest of India and Pakistan from the cold winds blowing from the north, but as the monsoon winds blow from the Indian sub-continent in the south, the winds are forced to rise over the Himalayas, dropping their rain and snow on the southern slopes. The northern slopes are in the rain shadow and receive very little rain.

The lower slopes of the southern Himalayas are more fertile. Terraces have been cut into the mountainside, and crops such as rice, sugar cane and maize are grown. Minerals are mined, hydroelectric power is produced and the trees are felled to make way for more crops, for fuel and to make paper products. However, the demand for wood and the cutting down of trees is having a disastrous effect on the lower slopes. The thin soil is being washed away from the upper slopes and into the rivers. Flooding is occurring in the valleys and plains below. To stop these things happening, more trees need to be planted.

Many followers of Buddhism live in high remote areas of the Himalayas. Mount Everest is a religious symbol to the Buddhists.

Discussing the photograph

▶ Explain to the children what the photograph shows.
▶ Describe the variety of climate experienced in the Himalayas and how the climate on the top of the peaks differs dramatically from that of the lower slopes (see above).
▶ Tell the children that many followers of Buddhism live in high remote areas of the Himalayas, because Mount Everest has religious importance to Buddhists.
▶ Can the children suggest what is in the foreground of the photograph? Explain that these are Buddhist prayer flags or prayer cloths. Prayers are written on the flags and Buddhists hope the good thoughts of the prayers will be carried away on the wind.
▶ Ask the children to imagine they are standing where the man is in the photograph. Ask them to describe what they can see, hear, feel.

Activities

▶ Using reference books, ask the children to find out about the six highest mountains in the Himalayas, stating how high they are and in which countries they are located.
▶ In the role of a climber, ask the children, in pairs, to write a short article for a newspaper about the weather conditions high in the Himalayas.
▶ In groups, ask the children to discuss what the difficulties of living in a mountainous area like the Himalayas would be. Ask the groups to feed back their views to the whole class.
▶ Ask the children to make up some prayers for peace and understanding in the world, and to write them on a prayer flag. String up the flags around the classroom.

Avalanche, Audio: Avalanche

An avalanche is the rapid movement of snow down a steep mountainside. Avalanches have always occurred in the mountainous regions, but with the growth of winter recreations, fatalities from avalanches have been on the rise since the 1950s.

MOUNTAIN ENVIRONMENTS

Many factors influence the occurrence of an avalanche, including the angle of the slope; snow factors, such as the size of grains, slab thickness and density; the terrain, such as the presence or absence of trees; and wind speed and direction. Ninety per cent of all avalanches occur on moderate slopes with an angle of 30° to 45° (snow tends not to accumulate on steeper slopes), the same slopes favoured by many skiers, snowboarders and snowmobilers. A change in temperature, a sudden warm, dry wind, and loud noises or vibrations are all that are necessary to trigger an avalanche.

The most hazardous type of avalanche is called a 'dry slab' avalanche. This occurs when a weak layer in the snow cover can no longer support new layers of snow above, causing the top layers to slide down the slope. On average, dry slab avalanches travel at about 100 to 130km per hour. The risks of an avalanche increase during major snowstorms and periods of thaw. Wind can gather up snow and deposit it ten times faster than snow falling from storms. This makes wind the most common weather-related cause of avalanches. Internationally, the Alpine countries of France, Austria, Switzerland, and Italy experience the greatest number of avalanches, and loss of life from them, annually.

This photograph shows an avalanche roaring down the mountain slopes in Switzerland. The impact of the rapid movement is clearly visible and the echo of the avalanche can be heard in the audio clip.

Discussing the photograph and sound

▶ Ask the children what the photograph shows.
▶ Discuss the reasons avalanches occur (see above).
▶ Play the audio clip of the avalanche while the children look at the photograph. Ask them to describe what they hear.

Activities

▶ Let the children find out more about avalanches, using reference books and the internet. Ask questions to focus their research, such as How do avalanches start? Where do they occur? Why do they occur? When do they occur?
▶ Ask the children to draw a series of diagrams to illustrate what they can hear on the audio clip and what they can see in the photograph.
▶ Ask the children, in groups, to debate and discuss ways to protect human life and property, and to minimise the impact of avalanches.
▶ Ask the children to close their eyes while you play the audio clip and to listen carefully. Then ask them to open their eyes and list their feelings.
▶ In pairs, tell the children to pretend they are tourists staying in a ski resort when the warning of an avalanche comes. Ask them to discuss and describe their feelings, and what they intend to do to protect themselves.
▶ Talk the children through the diagram of an avalanche on the 'Glaciers and avalanche' sheet on photocopiable page 24.

Aftermath of avalanche

The disastrous avalanche winter of 1950/1951 in the Swiss Alps resulted in 98 dead and 1500 damaged buildings. In February 1999, in the affected mountain areas, there were a similar number of avalanches. However, there were four times as many tourists and 1.5 times as many inhabitants but the avalanches claimed a similar number of lives. The fact that the damage was not worse was not just a matter of luck, but due to the development of a variety of avalanche protection programmes over the previous 50 years.

Avalanche prevention programmes involve a variety of methods, such as restrictions on building in areas where avalanches start and in their fall path; the construction of anti-avalanche barriers; avalanche early warning systems, and the closing and evacuating of areas; artificially started and controlled avalanches; reforestation and the maintenance of mountain forests to prevent avalanches starting; deflecting walls built to divert avalanche flows away from buildings and even entire villages and towns.

This photograph shows the village of Le Tour near Chamonix, in the French Alps, following the avalanche on Tuesday 9 February 1999, which killed 12 people. Two powerful avalanches hurtled down the mountain side onto this and another village, smashing and destroying 17 chalets and burying others under deep snow. Rescuers used sensors and dogs as they searched for survivors and for the dead. The frozen crust was so hardened by the end of the

MOUNTAIN ENVIRONMENTS

day that rescue workers had to resort to drills and heavy machinery to bore through it. Rescue work was hampered by overnight temperatures well below freezing, leaving rescuers little hope of finding anyone else alive under the snow and rubble. Anyone buried died of exposure if they had survived the blast of the avalanche, or died from suffocation from the powdery snow.

Discussing the photograph
▶ Explain to the children what this photograph shows (see above).
▶ Point out the twisted metal from smashed cars and splinters of wood from crushed chalets jutting out from hills of snow.
▶ Point out the heavy machinery the rescuers used to remove hundreds of tons of snow.
▶ Ask the children what angle the photograph was taken from (it's an aerial photograph).

Activities
▶ Ask the children to locate the French Alps and Chamonix on a map or in an atlas.
▶ Stick copies of the photograph in the centre of pieces of A3 paper and ask the children, in groups, to list what they can see in the photograph.
▶ Ask the children to write an account, in the style of a journalist, for an international newspaper about the avalanche in Chamonix. Ask them to produce an eye-catching title such as Killer Avalanche Sweeps Away Chalets.
▶ Ask the children, in pairs, to discuss and list ways that different governments are trying to minimise the impact of avalanches on life and property.

The largest glacier in Europe

This photograph shows sightseers at the snout of the Briksdal Glacier in Norway. It is an arm of the Jostedals glacier, the largest snowfield in Europe. The Jostedals glacier is a 500m^2 ice plateau that has 22 arms stretching down into nearby valleys. The clay particles of the meltwater give the local rivers and lakes their distinctive deep green colouring.

Glaciers are 'rivers' of ice, and like rivers they flow downhill, erode the landscape, transport material and deposit it. A glacier is an accumulation of ice, air, water and rock debris. It moves and flows very slowly downhill with gravity. The ice can be as large as a continent, such as the ice sheet covering Antarctica, or it can fill a small valley between two mountains – a valley glacier. Temperature and precipitation are the main ingredients for a glacier to develop and keep going. The temperature must be cold enough so that more ice accumulates than melts from the base or surface. The precipitation must be in the form of snow.

Glacial erosion changes the landscape in many ways, carving valleys, wearing away rock and stripping soil from the ground. Glaciers also add to the landscape by depositing materials. Glaciers pick up rocks in their path, smoothing the land over which they travel and dropping materials on their way. Glaciers have an almost limitless capacity for the size of rocks that they carry; they move more slowly than rivers, but they have more momentum. Glaciers erode because they move and carry debris at their base. Abrasion is caused by the scraping of material stuck in the glacier's base on the rock floor. As the ice moves over rock, it freezes large rocks into its base (small- and large-scale plucking) and carries them along as it moves. These rocks give the ice base a gritty texture, like a piece of sandpaper. The rocks scrape, or abrade, the underlying ground further. As ice passes over bedrock, abrasion can give it a polished look. Alternatively, large rocks in the ice can cut long scours in the base rock.

Ice sheets and glaciers act like conveyor belts. Most of the material eroded from under the ice sheet is carried toward the glacier's snout. As the material is eroded, it can be frozen into the lower part of the ice sheet and moved along, or it can be carried along just below the top of the ice sheet. Eventually, the eroded material is dumped at the glacier's snout. Depositional features are features created by the glacier depositing or releasing rocks and sediment. They vary in scale from thin ground cover to huge terminal moraines.

Discussing the photograph
▶ Explain to the children what the photograph shows.
▶ Ask the children to look closely at the snout of the glacier, where it is melting. Focus on the cracks and crevasses in the ice. Can they see the meltwater leaving the glacier?
▶ Tell the children that the Briksdal glacier is the most visited arm of the Jostedals glacier and a popular tourist destination.

MOUNTAIN ENVIRONMENTS

▶ Explain that the path to the snout of the glacier skirts waterfalls and weaves up river until the glacier is reached. Visitors have to be careful when visiting glaciers, as they are in constant motion (like rivers) and are potentially very dangerous.

Activities
▶ Ask the children to locate Norway, the Jostedals glacier and the Briksdal glacier on a map or in an atlas.
▶ Ask the children to find out, using reference books and the internet, how glaciers start and where they occur. Get them to include a sketch diagram of a glacier in their work.
▶ In groups, give the children holiday brochures and guide books. Ask them to find out about visits to glaciers and guided walks on them. Then ask them to design a visually appealing poster that could be used to advertise this type of holiday.
▶ In groups, ask the children to list the things (clothes and equipment) they think they should take in a rucksack for a guided walk on a glacier. Tell them to consider weather conditions, terrain, and so on.
▶ Give the children a copy of the 'Glaciers and avalanches' sheet on photocopiable page 24, and talk them through the glacier diagram.

Map of France, Diagram of Châtel

The French Alpine village of Châtel used to be a traditional farming village set at the head of the valley of the River Dranse close to the Swiss/French border. Its development into a ski resort has been carefully controlled and there are still working farms in the village. Châtel's beautiful scenery makes the entire area a haven for walkers and mountain bikers in the summer, and skiers in the winter.

Châtel is 50km from Geneva, the nearest international airport. To travel from Paris, there is a train to Thonon with a connecting bus service to Châtel. Access to Châtel is not always easy. Travel in high mountains is difficult. The roads are narrow and icy, and sometimes blocked by snow. Improving access (widening roads, building new tunnels, improving avalanche protection) is expensive.

Discussing the map and diagram
▶ Explain to the children that the village of Châtel is in the French Alps.
▶ Point out the location of Châtel and the French Alps on the 'Map of France'.
▶ Tell the children about Châtel. Over recent years, Châtel has developed into a winter ski resort and a favourite area for walkers and bikers in the summer.
▶ Tell the children that the the 'knife-sharp' mountain ridges are called arêtes and that these have been formed through glacial erosion. The upper parts of the mountains are always covered in snow and ice because the climate is cold and harsh at that altitude.
▶ Describe the variety of climate experienced in the Alps and how the climate on the top of the peaks differs dramatically from that of the lower slopes, especially in summertime. Explain how this impacts on how mountains are used at different altitudes.
▶ Explain to the children how the valley sides are very steep and rocky. In some places waterfalls cascade to the valley below.
▶ Explain to the children that the settlement of Châtel and the road are located on the flat valley floor. As with most Alpine villages, Châtel faces south (it is built mainly on the north side of the valley) so that the village receives most sunshine. The road along the valley floor is often closed in the winter due to heavy falls of snow or avalanches.
▶ Explain to the children that tourism (both in the winter and in the summer) is very important and brings in a lot of money, as tourists spend money on souvenirs, on ski lessons, equipment, ski lifts and accommodation. Ask the children to identify all the tourist facilities (ski lifts, bobsleigh runs etc.) shown on the diagram of the area around Châtel.

Activities
▶ Give the children a blank map of Europe. Ask them to locate and mark on their maps, using atlases, maps, and other reference material the following places: the French Alps; the River Dranse; Châtel; Geneva; Lake Geneva; Mont Blanc.
▶ Ask the children to find out how tourists may travel from the following places to Châtel: from Paris, France; from Turin, Italy; from Manchester, UK.

MOUNTAIN ENVIRONMENTS

▶ Ask the children, using the key on the diagram, to describe some of the features found in this area that are associated with the tourist industry. Would these features have been here when Châtel was simply a farming village?
▶ Ask the children to think about how life has changed for people who live and earn their living in the area around Châtel.

Châtel in winter, Skiing at Châtel

Over the past 30 years, many changes have occurred in Châtel to enable it to cater for the tourists who flock to the region. Châtel was a small, remote farming community. At first people came to the area to walk, climb and admire the scenery. In the 1970s and 1980s, winter sports (skiing, tobogganing, snowboarding, bobsleighing) became popular and Châtel become a 'winter playground' for tourists. The resort now caters for visitors all year round.

Châtel, at 1200m, has 41 lifts and 49 ski slopes. The type of skiing available suits all abilities, from beginners to advanced skiers. There are gentle, wide runs for beginners, sweeping tree-lined pistes for intermediates, and for the more experienced, runs which challenge and test both technique and nerve. Ski schools and childcare facilities are excellent, making Châtel an ideal destination for families. Châtel has two specially designed snow parks as well as a range of runs to challenge all snowboarders. For après-ski, Châtel has a selection of activities, including two high-tech cinemas, bowling and a natural ice rink. There are also numerous restaurants, bars and discos.

Discussing the photographs
▶ Show the children the photographs and ask what they think the images have in common. Explain that they both show views of Châtel following a large fall of snow.
▶ Tell the children that 'Châtel in winter' is a view of Châtel looking down from the mountainside.
▶ Ask the children to point out the main features in the photograph (a thick layer of snow covers the roofs of the chalets, a group of people are queuing for the chair lift, a few people are skiing down the slope, isolated coniferous trees can be seen on the lower slopes above the village and bare outcrops of rock protrude above the snow).
▶ Explain that the photograph 'Skiing at Châtel' is a view of Châtel looking southwards. Tell them that most Alpine villages are located on the valley floor or clinging to the lower slopes facing south. Villages tend to be on the north side of a valley so that they receive most sunlight.
▶ Ask the children to point out the main features in this photograph (a thick layer of snow covers the roofs of the chalets and the coniferous trees, large tracks of trees can be seen).
▶ Talk about the management of coniferous forests and reforestation as methods to prevent avalanches.

Activities
▶ Ask the children to use thought bubbles to describe how they would feel after climbing up the side of the valley and looking down on Châtel in the winter for the first time.
▶ In groups, ask the children to consider how the following people might feel about Châtel catering for visitors all year round: an elderly farmer, a young ski instructor, a middle-aged hotel owner, a retired elderly lady, an 11-year-old child.
▶ Copy both photographs and stick them in the middle of one sheet of A3 paper. Ask the children to label the physical features (in green) and human features (in blue).
▶ Penny, aged 12, and Jack, aged 9, are sending a postcard to their grandparents who have never visited an Alpine village in winter or skied. Ask the children to pretend to be either Penny or Jack, and to write a postcard describing their holiday in Châtel.
▶ Give the children the 'Ski resort word cards' on photocopiable page 23, and ask them to identify things that tourists could do at Châtel.

Châtel in summer

Châtel is an ideal resort for family holidays in the summer. Thousands of tourists visit mountain areas every year, to enjoy the clean, fresh air and the beautiful scenery. During the summer months several of the chair lifts and cable cars operate to provide easy access to the mountains and upper slopes for walkers and mountain bikers. The summer lift system allows

everyone to enjoy this breathtaking mountain scenery stretching along the border between France and Switzerland. There are over 200km of marked paths covering forests and high pastures, and more than 50 peaks to climb in a region stretching from Lake Geneva to Mont Blanc. June, July and August are the best months for walking and viewing the numerous Alpine flowers and the varied wildlife, such as golden eagles or chamois, which are native to this area.

Châtel offers many varied leisure activities, such as the summer toboggan runs, swimming, go-karting, horse riding, golf, rock climbing and water sports. The River Dranse offers some exciting white water, with grade 3-5 rapids. Other water sports include hydrospeed (an extreme sport of 'surfing' down a river with only a riverboard, flippers, safety helmet and a wetsuit!), rafting, Hot-Dog (an open-topped canoe for one or two people) and canyoning (a mixture of climbing and swimming following the course of the river over waterfalls and rockpools). Paragliding is also available and this provides an opportunity to glide effortlessly across this magnificent landscape and see the Alps from a bird's-eye view. Traditional summer festivals, such as the wood festival and the alpine pastures festival, are also held.

Discussing the photograph

▶ Explain to the children that this photograph is a view of Châtel taken from high up the valley side.
▶ Can the children suggest which season the photograph was taken in? Talk about the climatic conditions in summer (warm sunshine, clear blue skies, little rainfall).
▶ Ask the children to look carefully at the rich alpine pasture, the alpine flowers in the foreground, the coniferous forests and woodlands on the steeper slopes and the mountain peaks in the distance.
▶ Explain to the children the reasons why crops are not grown here (land too steep and unsuitable for farm machinery, soil too thin, climate too cold and wet, growing season too short).
▶ Ask the children to describe the physical and human features they can see in the photograph.

Activities

▶ In groups, ask the children to discuss what it would be like climbing up the side of the valley and looking down on Châtel in the summer. Ask questions to focus their discussion, such as: What would it be like standing on the top of the mountain? What could you see, hear, smell?
▶ In the same groups, ask the children to discuss how the view would be different from that seen in winter. Give the groups the photographs 'Châtel in winter' and 'Skiing at Châtel' (provided on the CD) to help them.
▶ Ask the children to research the mountain environment of the French Alps. Give them the following headings: Where is it? What is the landscape like? How can you get there? What do people in the area do? What are the reasons for the special character of this area? Ask the children to present their information as notes and bullet points.

The Lake District in the United Kingdom

The map shows the major mountain ranges in the United Kingdom. The Lake District National Park in the north west of England is the largest of England's National Parks. Its area of 2292km² covers mountains, high fells, lush green valleys and dales, woodlands, lakes, villages and quiet hamlets.

Although the Lake District countryside may seem wild, its appearance is due to human activity, particularly farming. People have been using the area for at least 10,000 years, and in 1951 it was designated as a National Park to protect it for future generations.

Discussing the map

▶ Explain to the children that this is a map of physical features of the United Kingdom, showing upland areas.
▶ Discuss the parts that make up the United Kingdom: Northern Ireland, Scotland, Wales and England. Can the children tell you their capital cities?
▶ Point out where the Lake District is on the map. Ask the children if they know which county the Lake District National Park is located in.

MOUNTAIN ENVIRONMENTS

Activities

▶ Give the children atlases and ask them to find out how upland areas are shown on them.
▶ As a class, locate the highest peaks in each of the countries of the United Kingdom on an atlas. (Ben Nevis (1343m) in Scotland, Snowdon (1085m) in Wales, Slieve Donard, County Down (852m) in Northern Ireland and Scafell Pike (978m) in England.)
▶ Give the children an outline map showing the upland areas of the UK, without labels, and an atlas. Ask the children to label the following upland areas: North West Highlands, Grampians, Southern Uplands, Cheviot Hills, Cumbrian Mountains, Pennines, North York Moors, Cambrian Mountains, Brecon Beacons, Exmoor, Dartmoor, Antrim Mountains, Mourne Mountains and the highest peaks in each of the countries (see previous activity).

OS map of the Lake District

This map is part of the Ordnance Survey (OS) Landranger Series, Map 90, showing the area around Grasmere, Ambleside and Elterwater. Maps are drawn to scale, some showing a small area in detail, while others show a large area in outline. The scale of this map is 1:50 000 (one to fifty thousand), which means for every 1cm on the map, there are 50,000cm on the ground. Simple symbols are used to show buildings, roads, woodlands etc. The symbols on an OS map are known as conventional signs, because they are used by convention or agreement by everyone. Straightforward guides to using the OS maps and symbols can be found on the OS website at http://www.ordnancesurvey.co.uk/oswebsite/education/free.

This map shows an upland and mountainous area. Brown contour lines are used on OS maps to show height and gradient. Contour lines join places of equal height: the closer the contour lines, the steeper the slope. Spot heights are used to show peaks.

Discussing the map

▶ Explain to the children that this is part of an OS Landranger map with a scale 1:50 000 and tell them what this map shows.
▶ Discuss the function of the Ordnance Survey and why it is important to have accurately drawn maps.
▶ Explain to the children what contour lines are and how they are used to show the steepness and height of land.
▶ Draw attention to the symbols on the map and discuss the use of conventional symbols.
▶ Ask the children to discuss how the map shows physical and human features and to describe the physical features that dominate the map.
▶ Ask the children if they would like to live in Grasmere, and encourage them to give reasons for their answers.
▶ Ask the children what they notice about the routes the roads take and how the terrain affects them. Why do they not cross the mountains?

Activities

▶ Ask the children, using the conventional symbols for Landranger 1:50 000 map, to list and describe the amenities located in Grasmere and Ambleside.
▶ Ask the children to find out how to use contour lines and spot heights. Encourage them to look at how the gradients of the roads are shown.
▶ Settlements are located in the valleys or on lower slopes. Ask the children to use the map and reference materials to explain why this is. Encourage them to consider factors such as weather conditions and accessibility for transport.
▶ Ask the children to undertake research on National Parks in the United Kingdom.

Grasmere

Grasmere is a traditional village situated in the heart of the Lake District National Park. Grasmere consists of a cluster of grey stone houses on the old packhorse road, which runs beside the River Rothay. The rocky peak of the 'Lion and the Lamb' towers over the village. Grasmere is centrally situated for visitors who want a challenge and wish to take on the craggy peaks of the Scafell Pikes, Helvellyn, Skiddaw and the Langdale Pikes.

In the foreground of the photograph, to the south of the village, is Grasmere lake. The lake is 23m deep. Grasmere was once the home of the poet William Wordsworth, who described

the lake as 'The most loveliest spot that man hath found.' Tourists can visit two of his former homes: Dove Cottage, his home from 1799 to 1808 and where he wrote some of his best poetry, and Rydal Mount, his home from 1813 until his death in 1850. William Wordsworth and members of his family are buried in St Oswald's churchyard in the centre of Grasmere.

Discussing the photograph
▶ Explain to the children that this photograph shows Grasmere, a traditional village in the heart of the Lake District National Park.
▶ Tell the children that the lake in the foreground of the photograph is Grasmere lake.
▶ Explain that the photograph shows the area in early autumn. Ask the children to notice some of the features in the photograph (the lake, flat valley bottom and the craggy peaks with snow on the top).

Activities
▶ Using the 'OS map of the Lake District' (provided on the CD), ask the children to locate Grasmere.
▶ In groups, ask the children to use thought bubbles to describe how they would feel when they reached the top of one of the peaks and looked at the view over Grasmere and the lake.
▶ In pairs, ask the children to research and investigate this mountain environment under the following headings: Where is it? What is the landscape like? How can you get there? Why is this place special? Ask the children to present their information either in a poster or as a PowerPoint presentation.
▶ Give each child a copy of the weather forecast for hilly areas in the Lake District. Ask them to underline all the weather words. Then in groups, ask the children to write the script for a short factual news report, highlighting how weather conditions can enhance or detract from tourism in an area.

Farmhouse near Grasmere

This photograph shows a hill farm on the lower slopes near Grasmere. The land slopes steeply, and the soil is thin and unsuitable for crops. The grass is short and coarse making it only suitable for sheep and goats to graze. The small fields are divided by dry-stone walls, the stones originally having been removed from the field.

Life on hill farms in the UK today is hard. Huge numbers of sheep are reared on the hill farms and moorlands of Cumbria. The sheep population of Cumbria was around three million before the Foot and Mouth outbreak in 2001. Hardy breeds are favoured, breeds that can withstand the cold winds and bitter winters. The North Country Mule is a crossbred sheep common in Cumbria. On the lower fields of Cumbria, dairy cattle are kept in large numbers and butter production is important in the county. Cumberland rum butter is a delicious local speciality of butter flavoured with rum, sugar and spices. Goats and sheep are widely farmed for their milk, too, which is increasingly used for making yoghurt and cheese.

The rural economy of the Lakeland Fells relies heavily on agriculture and tourism. Many hill farms offer bed and breakfast and/or self-catering facilities (cottages, caravans and camping). Some offer tea room facilities. Local produce includes meats, game, wool, timber, fish, wool insulation, eggs, herbal products, ice cream and crafts. A farm shop is located at Holker Hall and there is the National Drystone Walling Centre. Major supermarkets in the area promote local produce and the locally owned M6 motorway services at Tebay have a farm shop and serve local produce.

Discussing the photograph
▶ Can the children suggest what sort of building the photograph shows? Explain that it is a hill farm on the lower slopes near Grasmere.
▶ Ask the children to notice how the land slopes steeply and explain that the soil is thin. Focus on how short and coarse the grass is, and that the fields are small and unsuitable for a lot of farm machinery. Explain that these are reasons why crops are not being grown here.
▶ Discuss with the children what a hill farm produces (see above) and how many farmers are now supplementing their income with other activities (see above).
▶ Ask the children to describe the physical and human features they can see.

▶ Discuss the seasons and different types of weather experienced in the Lake District. Discuss how the weather might change suddenly in mountainous areas.

Activities
▶ Ask the children to list what type of clothes and equipment they think they should take if they went for a walk in a mountainous area.
▶ In pairs, ask the children to look at the photograph and imagine they got lost there. Ask them to consider the following questions: How would you feel? What would you do? How do you think you would feel when you were found? How do you think your parents/carers would feel when they realised you were missing, and then when you were found?
▶ Ask the children to write guidelines for a successful camping trip into a mountainous environment in the Lake District.
▶ Give the children the 'Ski resort word cards' on photocopiable page 23. Ask them to identify things that they could do in Grasmere.

Sarah Nelson's gingerbread shop

Sarah Nelson is a famous name associated with the village of Grasmere. Grasmere Gingerbread, made since 1854 following Sarah Nelson's original recipe, is still made and sold here. The shop has become an attraction in itself. It is tucked away at the corner of the churchyard of St Oswald's Church. The wonderful smell of piping hot, freshly baked gingerbread has attracted generations of tourists to the shop.

The rural economy of the Lakeland Fells relies heavily on agriculture and tourism. Thousands of tourists visit the Lake District every year, to enjoy the clean fresh air and the beautiful scenery. The village of Grasmere offers accommodation, including many hotels and bed and breakfast facilities. There are several tea rooms, cafes and craft shops. Local produce, including meats, fish, wool, herbal products, ice cream and crafts are sold, too.

Discussing the photograph
▶ Explain to the children that the photograph shows the Grasmere Gingerbread Shop as it is today. It was built in 1630, originally as the village school. Tell the children about the shop's popularity.
▶ Discuss with the children the materials the shop is made of and the size of the building.
▶ Apart from gingerbread, what else do the children think might be sold in the shop?

Activities
▶ In groups, ask the children to discuss why they think tourism can be both good and bad for an area and why. Tell them to draw up lists of the positive effects (creates jobs, brings in income) and the negative effects (increases litter, pollution, congestion on the roads).
▶ Give the children holiday brochures of the Lake District to look at and ask them to list images that holiday brochures don't show.
▶ In groups, ask the children to think about and make lists of what makes a 'good' holidaymaker and a 'bad' holidaymaker. As a class, compare lists and then ask each child to draw a cartoon strip that shows examples of good and bad behaviour by holidaymakers.

NOTES ON THE PHOTOCOPIABLE PAGES

Word cards PAGE 22-23

These cards show key words that the children will encounter when working on this unit. They include:
▶ words relating to climate and terrain
▶ words describing tourist activities in Alpine regions.

The 'Mountain word cards' support the specific study of mountain environments. Encourage the children to think of other appropriate words to add to them in order to build up a word bank on mountain environments. They could also use the word cards in displays using the maps and photographs from the Resource Gallery, and to help them in talking and writing about the images.

MOUNTAIN ENVIRONMENTS

Activities
▶ Make copies of the word cards, laminate them and cut them out. They could be used for the children to play word games and spelling games, or let the children invent their own games.
▶ In pairs, ask the children to sort the 'Mountain word cards' into categories (such as weather and terrain).
▶ Ask the children, in pairs, to make a crossword puzzle that contains words related to weather and to tourist activities in mountains.
▶ Ask the children to sort the 'Ski resort word cards' into winter and summer activities.
▶ Give the children travel brochures and ask them to find destinations throughout the world where tourists can undertake the activities.
▶ In pairs, ask the children to make a word search about mountain environments.
▶ Ask the children to make their own illustrated dictionary or glossary for the unit.

Glaciers and avalanches PAGE 24

Use the diagram of the glacier on this sheet with the photograph 'The largest glacier in Europe' (provided on the CD) and see the notes for that photograph for further information on glaciers.

Use the diagram of the avalanche in conjunction with the photographs of 'Avalanche' and 'Aftermath of avalanche' (provided on the CD) and see the notes for these photographs for more information on avalanches.

Activities
▶ Talk the children through the diagrams.
▶ Ask the children to find out about glaciers. How do glaciers start? Where do they occur? Why do they occur? When do they occur?
▶ Ask the children to draw their own sketch diagram of a glacier, labelling it as appropriate.
▶ Give the children an outline of the avalanche diagram without the labels and ask them to label it.

Mountain climber PAGE 25

This photocopiable resource shows an illustration of a climber in all the clothing and with the equipment required for climbing a mountain.

Activities
▶ Discuss the sheet with the children and talk about the climber's equipment.
▶ Print off enough copies of the photograph 'Climbing Everest' (provided on the CD) for the children to work in groups, and enough copies of the illustration of the climber for each child. Ask the children to talk about what is happening in the photograph and the equipment the climber needs to climb Mount Everest. Explain that in addition, climbers climbing Mount Everest have to carry oxygen in bottles with them, as the air is thin.
▶ Ask the children to match the labels to the equipment shown on photocopiable sheet.

Mountain word cards

MOUNTAIN ENVIRONMENTS

blizzard	summit
snowstorm	terrain
avalanche	altitude
snowline	Alpine
snowdrift	forest
weather	tourism
precipitation	landscape
season	mountain

Ski resort word cards

MOUNTAIN ENVIRONMENTS

skiing
tobogganing
snowboarding
bobsleighing
viewing the scenery
walking
mountain biking
rock climbing

Glaciers and avalanches

Glaciers

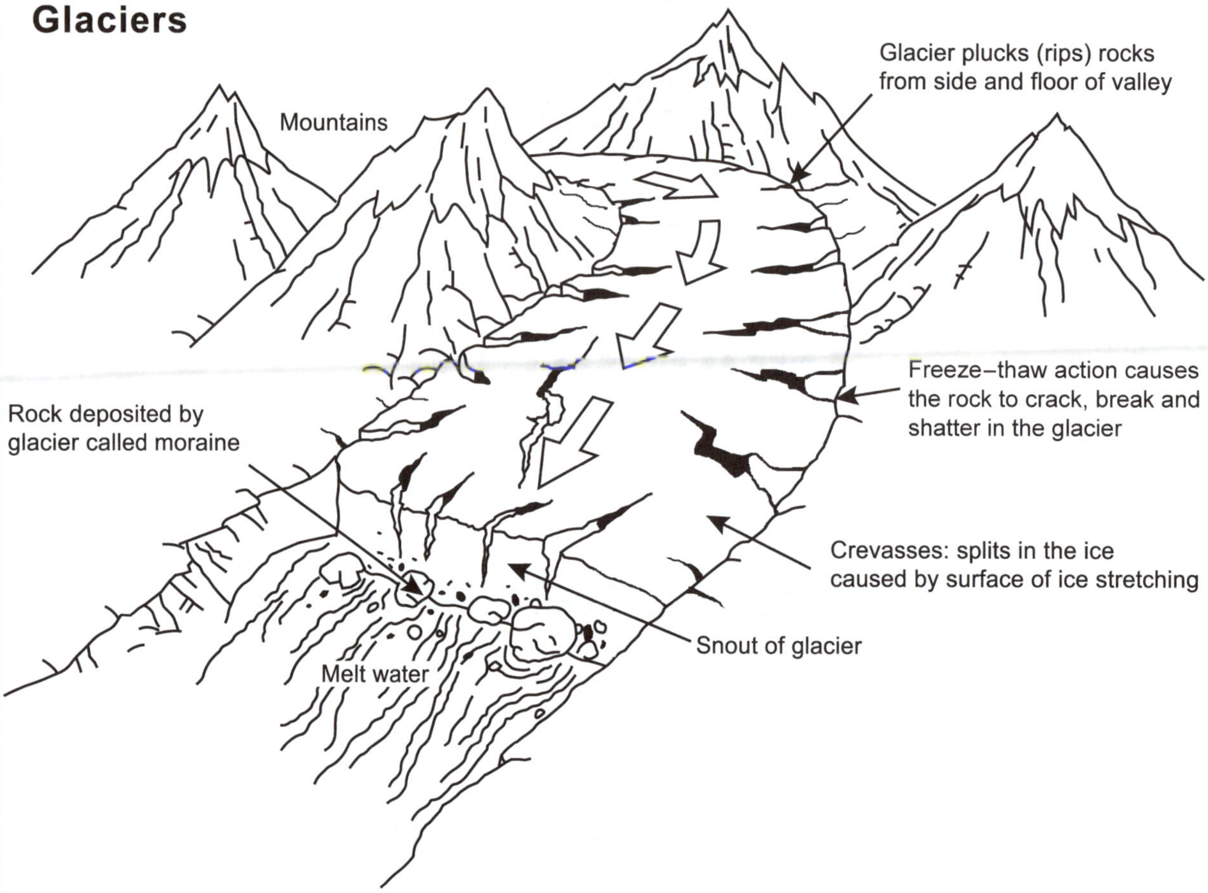

- Mountains
- Glacier plucks (rips) rocks from side and floor of valley
- Freeze–thaw action causes the rock to crack, break and shatter in the glacier
- Rock deposited by glacier called moraine
- Crevasses: splits in the ice caused by surface of ice stretching
- Snout of glacier
- Melt water

Avalanches

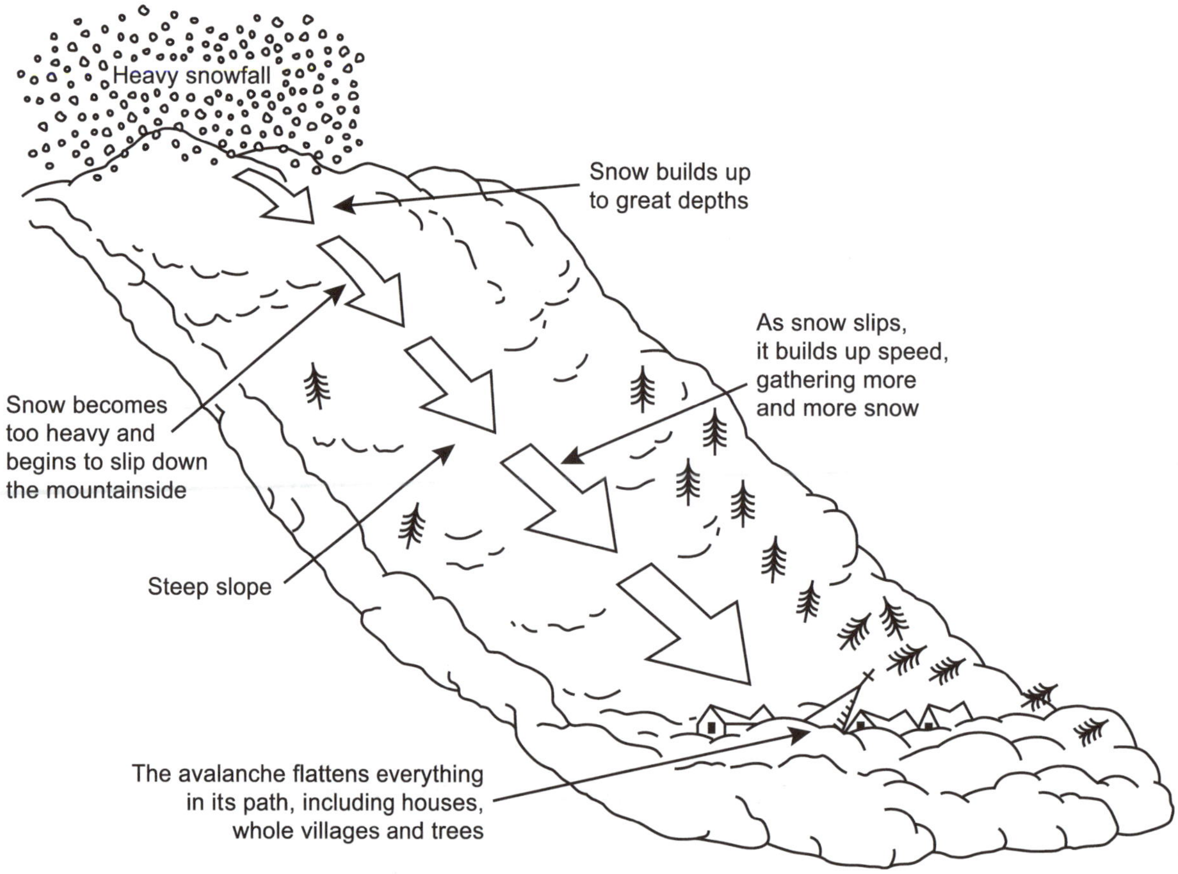

- Heavy snowfall
- Snow builds up to great depths
- Snow becomes too heavy and begins to slip down the mountainside
- As snow slips, it builds up speed, gathering more and more snow
- Steep slope
- The avalanche flattens everything in its path, including houses, whole villages and trees

Mountain climber

MOUNTAIN ENVIRONMENTS

- Cut out the labels and match them to the diagram.

insulated, waterproof and windproof parka	boots	insulated gloves
crampons	insulated, waterproof and windproof pants	balaclava
goggles	helmet	ice axe
ropes and harness	backpack	trekking pole

COASTS

Content and skills

The content in this chapter supports the activities in unit 23, 'Investigating coasts', of the QCA Scheme of Work for geography at Key Stage 2. It supports the unit by providing some necessary resources for exploring ideas related to water and how it affects people and landscapes.

The content supplements and extends the unit by exploring different coastal environments and how the power of the sea plays a major part in shaping the landscape. Coastal features caused by erosion and by deposition are explored, and the ways in which coastal areas are used and protected are investigated. The Purbeck coast in Dorset is used for many of the examples and a locator map of the coast is provided. This area has been used because the examples are good and nearly every stage in the development of both erosional and depositional features can be found there.

Resources on the CD-ROM

The resources include a map, video footage and ground-level photographs. Through the use of these good quality secondary resources, alongside independent research using ICT and other resources, the children will develop a good understanding of the close relationship between coastal areas and people. The resources reflect a balance of approach, so that an understanding of the physical processes and human development are explored side by side.

Photocopiable pages

The photocopiable resources within the book will enable children to develop geographical vocabulary associated with the work and power of the sea, know about different stages in the formation of erosional and depositional landforms, and develop an understanding of how coastal areas are used for pleasure and for work. They are also provided in PDF format on the CD and can be printed from there. They include:
- ▶ word cards relating to landforms formed by deposition
- ▶ word cards to support the description of amenities and types of accommodation found in seaside resorts
- ▶ a labelling exercise for children to recognise coastal features caused by erosion
- ▶ a matching activity to understand the different methods of protecting the coast from erosion.

Geographical skills

Skills developed by activities using the resources in this chapter include those of map reading and interpretation, identification of key features within visual images and the development of the relevant geographical vocabulary. Geographical enquiry is promoted and children are encouraged to ask geographical questions, collect and analyse the evidence and draw conclusions. Children are encouraged to identify and explain the different demands and requirements people have regarding the use of coastal areas. Knowledge and understanding of places is developed, as children locate coastal areas, describe where the places are, why they are like they are, and how and why places change over time. Children's understanding of how people can either improve and manage coastal areas sustainably, or damage them, is developed through investigation.

NOTES ON THE CD-ROM RESOURCES

Map of the Purbeck coast

A coast is the edge of the land where it meets the sea or ocean. A coastline is the outline of the land. The United Kingdom is surrounded by sea and has thousands of kilometres of coastline. In the UK, it is impossible to live more than 160km from the sea. The coasts around Britain are very varied and are changing all the time. There are beaches, cliffs, sand dunes, sandy bays, salt marshes and estuaries. In some coastal areas the action of the waves is wearing away the land (erosion) and in other parts the action of the waves is adding material to the land (deposition).

Beaches are made of particles of rock deposited by the sea, and can be flat and sandy, or steeper and made of pebbles (shingle). They are covered and uncovered each day by the sea, as the tides come in and go out. Where the land is steep or there is a nearly vertical rock face at the edge of the land, cliffs are formed.

The coastal features located on the Purbeck coast in Dorset result from the way the power of the sea has acted on rocks of different resistance. Every stage in the development of bays and headlands can be seen around this area.

Discussing the map

▶ Explain to the children that this map shows the coastal area between Chesil Beach and Christchurch on the southern coast of England.
▶ Ask the children to describe the shape of the coastline.
▶ Remind the children of the directions of the compass and ask them to describe where places are in relation to each other. For example, Lulworth Cove is to the east of Durdle Door, and Weymouth is north of Portland Harbour.

Activities

▶ Ask the children what a coast is. Agree the most accurate definition.
▶ Using a map of the British Isles and an atlas, ask the children to locate places they have visited on the coast. Encourage them to use the indexes (page and grid reference).
▶ Ask the children to collect pictures of different kinds of coastline. Locate each coastal area and make a class display. Ask the children to write a caption for each picture.
▶ Enlarge the map and print all the photographs in the Resource Gallery that relate to this area. Make a class display, locating each feature on the map.

Hengistbury Head

This photograph shows Hengistbury Head, which lies to the eastern end of Poole Harbour near Bournemouth, on the south coast of England. Hengistbury Head is a 36m high sandstone headland, at the end of a 1km long peninsula. The original formation of Hengistbury Head dates back approximately 60 million years. The area contains an Ancient Monument (the Double Dykes) and some historians refer to it as the first urban settlement in England.

Protecting the area from erosion by the sea has been an issue for many years. Millions of pounds have been spent, developing and deploying many different methods of protection, such as groynes and marram grass. Sand dunes have formed where sand has been blown off the beach and a bank of sand has piled up. Marram grass is specially adapted to grow through shifting sands. The stems and roots of marram grass trap the sand and help slow its movement.

Hengistbury Head is an environmentally sensitive area, with a Nature Reserve and many rare plants, birds and animals. It is an important site for breeding and migratory birds, and the area is designated a Site of Special Scientific Interest (SSSI).

Discussing the photograph

▶ Ask the children to describe what physical and human features they can see in the photograph. (In the foreground there are sand dunes, marram grass, heathland and scrub. In the distance, there are groynes, which have been deployed to prevent the sand from being eroded away.)
▶ Explain to the children how sand dunes are formed, why they are important and how they can be protected (see above).

COASTS

▶ Tell the children about Hengistbury Head's special status (SSSI). What do they think this means? What do they think needs to be protected in an area like this? What kind of action could be taken?

Activities
▶ Ask the children to locate Hengistbury Head on the 'Map of the Purbeck coast' (provided on the CD).
▶ In groups, ask the children to put forward a case for one of the following: (a) for letting Hengistbury Head erode away naturally so the local council don't waste any more money protecting it, or (b) to build more groynes. Hold a class debate.
▶ In pairs, ask the children to write a letter to the local council explaining why they think it is important that Hengistbury Head should be protected.

COASTAL FEATURES FORMED BY EROSION

Cove

Waves have the power to erode and break up rocks over time. Their power depends on their height and this is affected by the speed of the wind and the length of time the wind has been blowing over the sea. The greater the distance (the fetch) over which the wind has been able to blow across the water, the more powerful the waves.

The processes of coastal erosion are relatively simple, but the impact and patterns of erosion are complex because of a wide number of factors, including rock type and structure, beach nature, fetch and currents. Erosion includes hydraulic action (the breaking of the waves on the cliffs), abrasion as a result of corrasion (the process where pebbles and sand are flung against cliffs, wearing away the rock), and attrition (the process where erosion continues by grinding down the cliff fall material). Weathering also contributes to the breakdown of rocks on the cliff through physical weathering (freeze–thaw action) and chemical weathering (dissolving the rocks).

The horseshoe bay of Lulworth Cove, in the photograph, was formed by the sea's erosive power. Along this coast there is a band of limestone, which forms a relatively resistant barrier against the sea. However, at this point, a small stream used to reach the sea through a break in the hard limestone rock. This breach allowed the sea to erode not only the limestone, but to enter the valley and erode the less resistant softer rocks (clay and sandstone) behind. Rapid erosion took place. When the sea reached the next thick band of rock (chalk), erosion slowed because the thickness of the chalk formed a resistant cliff at the back of the bay.

Discussing the photograph
▶ Explain to the children that the land around the coast is made up of different types of rock, some more resistant than others.
▶ Discuss with the children why bays are formed in some areas, because the rock is softer and erodes more quickly.
▶ Tell the children that the photograph shows a horseshoe-shaped bay on the south coast of England called Lulworth Cove. Explain how this bay was formed.
▶ Point out the thick chalk cliffs at the back of the cove. Explain why these resisted erosion.

Activities
▶ Ask the children to locate Lulworth Cove on the 'Map of the Purbeck coast' (provided on the CD). Ask each child to draw and label a sketch map of the area in the photograph.
▶ Ask the children to draw diagrams to explain the way that coves are formed.

Coastal arches
Cliffs are eroded more rapidly in some places than others. A headland is formed where there is an area of harder, more resistant rock and the waves erode it on both sides. If there is a softer rock, or one with more cracks and joints in it, the sea will erode it much faster than where the rock is more resistant. Eventually caves may form. Sometimes, as caves are enlarged through erosion by the sea, they continue to be eroded from both sides, until eventually they may be eroded right through. This looks a bit like a bridge with an arch of rock over the top, so it is called an 'arch'.

COASTS

This photograph shows the view of Durdle Door in Dorset. Durdle Door is a natural coastal arch located about half-a-mile west of Lulworth Cove. Note the comparitive whiteness of the limestone.

Discussing the photograph
- Ask the children to describe the feature they can see in the photograph.
- Explain to the children that the photograph is of Durdle Door, Dorset. It is an example of a coastal arch, which has been formed by erosion.
- Explain how the arch is formed (see above).
- Encourage the children to look carefully at the structure of the rock and rock layers, and notice how the rock layers have been tilted until they are almost vertical.

Activities
- Ask the children to locate Durdle Door on the 'Map of the Purbeck coast' (provided on the CD).
- Ask the children to draw and label a field sketch of the photograph.
- Give the children a copy of 'Coastal features caused by erosion' on photocopiable page 43.
- Ask the children to draw and label a sequence of diagrams to show how a coastal arch is formed.

Stacks and stumps

Stacks are isolated upstanding rocks that are formed by erosion. Wave action pounds away at a rock barrier, such as a headland. First, it attacks weaknesses such as joints and cracks, eroding a cave on the headland. The cave is deepened until it passes all the way through the headland to form an arch. As erosion continues, the arch of rock will get thinner and weaker until (usually during a storm) it collapses, leaving a large rock standing in the sea. This is called a stack. Eventually the upstanding stack is eroded to form a stump.

The photograph shows Old Harry Rocks off the Purbeck coast in Dorset, an example of an isolated stack. Other examples of stacks and stumps include The Needles, which are located off the Isle of Wight. The Needles are blocks of chalk that have been eroded over time by the sea. Much of the erosion is gradual, but sometimes there are dramatic events. In 1764, a fourth Needle, which was 37m tall and known as 'Lot's wife', collapsed into the sea. The crash was heard many kilometres away.

Discussing the photograph
- Ask the children to describe what they see in the photograph.
- Tell the children that the photograph shows an example of stacks called Old Harry Rocks. Explain how they were formed.
- How do the children think the stacks used to be connected to the mainland? Talk about what it would have looked like in the various stages of erosion.

Activities
- Ask the children to locate Old Harry Rocks on the 'Map of the Purbeck coast' (provided on the CD).
- Ask the children to draw and label a sequence of diagrams to show how a cave, an arch and then a stack are formed. For less able children, provide an outline sketch of the process and/or labels to attach.
- Let the children use maps and atlases to locate where there are other examples of caves, arches and stacks around the coast of the British Isles. For example, The Needles. Ask the children to plot these features on an outline map, using symbols to represent them.

COASTAL FEATURES FORMED BY DEPOSITION

Bars and spits

The prevailing wind blows the waves towards the shore at an angle, so a wave rolls up the beach diagonally from the direction the wind is blowing and takes the sand and pebbles with it. Instead of flowing back in the same direction it came from, the wave goes straight back

down the beach, and any pebbles and sand carried by the wave roll straight down the beach, at right angles to the shore, with the backwash. The sand and pebbles carried by the waves thus travel along the shore in a zigzag fashion. This is called longshore drift.

When something causes the waves to change their speed and/or move more slowly, they don't have enough energy to carry all the sand and shingle. The waves then drop (deposit) any material they are carrying. In time, these deposits may pile high and can form a ridge, which may grow out from the shore. This is called a spit. Examples are found at Spurn Head in East Yorkshire and Hurst Castle Spit in Hampshire. If a ridge is formed, which lies approximately parallel to the coast, it is called a bar. The shallow water behind a bar is called a lagoon.

The photograph shows Chesil Beach in Dorset, which is the longest bar in Europe, stretching from West Bay to the Isle of Portland, a distance of approximately 29km. A bar that joins an island to the mainland is called a tombolo, so Chesil Beach is an example of a tombolo, because it joins the Isle of Portland to the mainland. Chesil Beach encloses a lagoon called The Fleet, which is the largest tidal (saltwater) lagoon in Britain at 13km long.

Discussing the photograph

▶ Explain to the children what longshore drift is and illustrate with diagrams showing how it occurs.
▶ Tell the children that the photograph shows Chesil Beach, Dorset, and the enclosed lagoon, the Fleet. Explain how the bar formed (see above).
▶ Point out how Chesil Beach joins the Isle of Portland to the mainland.
▶ Ask the children, in groups, to look at the photograph and describe what they can see. What physical features are evident? Ask the groups to share their findings with the class.

Activities

▶ Ask the children to locate Chesil Beach on the 'Map of the Purbeck coast' (provided on the CD).
▶ Ask the children to draw and label a field sketch of the photograph. Remind them to give the field sketch a title.
▶ In pairs, ask one child to explain how a bar is formed. Ask the other child to make notes from the first child's explanation, and then discuss a selection of children's notes with the rest of the class.
▶ Use the 'Deposition word cards' on photocopiable page 41 for the children to familiarise themselves with key words about Chesil Beach.

EROSION

Barton-on-Sea cliff face, Warning sign

Barton-on-Sea is part of the town of New Milton, Hampshire, and is built on a cliff of clay. The cliff has been eroding rapidly over many years (up to 1m per year). This rapid rate of erosion happens because of the powerful and destructive waves, the longshore drift from west to east, dredging offshore and also the groyne systems to the west in Bournemouth, which starves Barton beach. Many schemes have been undertaken to protect the cliffs, including drainage, revetments, riprap at the foot of the cliff.

The cliff is unstable because of the erosion at its foot. Too little material was being brought from the west to create beaches that would protect the cliff. In February 1974, during a very bad storm, the revetment was breached, damaging 200m of the cliff foot defences. During November, in the same year, the cliff and revetment began to collapse. In the following spring (1975), more erosion took place and several houses were lost.

To the west of the town there is a fairly heavily defended stretch of coastline, with groynes, revetments and cliff draining works. These have slowed the erosion, protecting the valuable properties located there. However, to the east of the town it is difficult to introduce an effective coastal protection programme. The properties on the top of the cliffs are mainly holiday chalets which are of relatively low value. The management strategy adopted is simply to pick them up and move them backwards when they get within an unsafe distance of the cliff top.

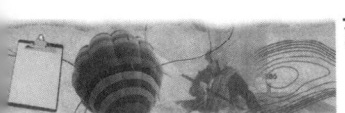

COASTS

Discussing the photographs
▶ Explain to the children where Barton-on-Sea is and why the cliffs are so unstable.
▶ Ask the children to look at the photograph 'Warning sign'. Discuss what the sign says and why they think it is used.
▶ Using the photographs of Barton-on-Sea, ask the children why they think people built buildings on top of the cliff. Were the buildings actually built close to the edge? If not, can they explain what has happened?
▶ Describe the type of coastal defences that have been used to try to protect this area.

Activities
▶ Ask the children to write an account explaining why some areas of cliff are being protected, while others are not.
▶ Let the children look at the Barton-on-Sea official website (www.bartononsea.org.uk) to view more images of the coastline. Ask the children to write to a penpal, describing Barton-on-Sea, reminding them to talk about the coastal features.

Collapse of a cliff

On some coasts there is a lot of erosion. Waves push sand or pebbles against the cliffs, slowly wearing them away. A cliff may be undercut or worn away at the bottom, causing it to collapse in a rockfall or landslide (where large masses of rock slip or fall onto the beach). The Yorkshire coast is famous for rapid erosion. Waves from the North Sea hit the lower parts of the soft-boulder clay cliffs with very strong force, causing the soft rock to be worn away at a rate of 2m per year.

Holbeck Hotel, a four-star hotel, was built in 1880 in the South Cliff area of Scarborough, Yorkshire. It stood some 65m above sea level. The building was separated by an extensive lawn from the edge of a 'small cliff', a gentle grassy slope, criss-crossed with public paths, running down to a much steeper face for the final 12m drop to sea level.

In June 1993, the upper part of the cliff slipped downwards, the lawn disappeared and the ground collapsed under the whole of the seaward wing of the hotel. The massive landslip took place in four stages. First, on the evening of Thursday 3 June 1993, the slope slipped downwards. Then, in the early morning of Friday 4 June, the second stage of the landslip removed two-thirds of the lawn. By 7.45am guests and staff were evacuated (no one was hurt). That afternoon the third stage took the failure back to the main front wall of the building, removing the conservatory, and on Sunday 6 June the final stage occurred, involving almost the entire seaward wing of the main building. The remainder of the hotel was unsafe and had to be demolished.

Discussing the photograph
▶ Discuss with the children what is happening. Can they explain why?
▶ Discuss with the children why they think people built this building so close to the sea, in an area where erosion was happening. Explain that no one thought that the sea would erode the coast as quickly as it has in Yorkshire.

Activities
▶ Encourage the children to research the Holbeck Hotel incident further. Focus their research with questions, such as: On which coast of Britain was the hotel? How many metres of the coast are wearing away per year there? How high above sea level was the hotel?
▶ In pairs, ask the children to retell the incident in their own words. Record their retelling.
▶ In groups, ask the children to role-play being guests and employees of the hotel, speaking to a TV reporter on the night of 3 June 1993. What might they have heard, felt and seen?

PROTECTING THE COAST

Groynes

Groynes are fences made out of wood, concrete, steel or stone. Most groynes are made of tropical hardwood (as shown in the photograph), because this wood can resist erosion. Groynes are built at right angles to the shore and run down the beach into the sea. They have

been constructed on many beaches around the British coastline, and are designed to trap material and slow down the rate of longshore drift. They reduce the impact of the waves on the beach, and sand or shingle piles up on the side of the groyne facing the prevailing wind. By forming a larger beach area, they stop the waves from attacking the cliffs behind the beach. Groynes can also stop longshore drift from blocking small harbours. Groynes, however, are expensive to build (they cost over £250,000 each) and are expected to last about 20 years. In some areas, groynes have been blamed for the rise in erosion rates further down the coast.

The photograph shows an example of a groyne at Llandudno, North Wales. Llandudno is on a peninsula, which juts out into the North Sea. Llandudno lies between two limestone headlands, the Great Orme and the Little Orme.

Discussing the photograph
▶ Explain to the children that the photograph shows an example of a wooden groyne, erected with others to prevent beach erosion.
▶ Ask the children how they think groynes protect the coastline.
▶ Explain to the children that groynes can be made of wood, concrete or stone and extend from the shore into the sea.

Activities
See the activities for 'A revetment', below.

A revetment

This photograph is of the revetment at Snettisham beach, in Norfolk. It is a slope made of concrete, which works by breaking up and absorbing the energy of the waves. Revetments are fairly costly to build and can look unsightly. The lorry is adding extra sand to top up the 'thin' beach, while the other vehicle spreads the sand. Adding sand and shingle to beaches is called beach nourishment. However, this will continue to need replacing and topping up, as some sand will be lost due to natural wave movement.

Discussing the photograph
▶ Explain to the children what the photograph shows (see above) and how revetments work to protect the coast.
▶ Ask the children what they think the two vehicles are doing. Explain to them what beach nourishment is (see above).

Activities
▶ As a class, list the advantages and disadvantages of building a sea wall instead of the other two methods of protecting the coast shown in the photographs (groynes and revetments).
▶ Role-play a decision by the local council to allow the sea to flood an area because it is too costly to protect it with other measures. Divide the children into six groups to represent the following roles: a local wildlife expert, a local caravan park owner, a local resident, the Mayor of the council, a farmer who owns land, a tourist. Ask each group (in role) to list three statements about the impact this decision will have on their lives. Then ask the children to form six new groups, each comprising one representative from the original groupings. In their new groups, still in role, ask the children to give views and discuss their statements, to listen to the views of others and to consider whether their view has changed.
▶ Give the children a copy of 'Protecting the coast' on photocopiable page 44, to support their understanding of groynes and revetments.

Dykes

The Netherlands is made partly of land reclaimed from the waters of the North Sea. Today, approximately 27 per cent of the Netherlands is actually below sea level. Over 60 per cent of the country's population live in this area. The lowland of the Netherlands is enclosed by embankments (stone or earthen walls) known as dykes, constructed as a defence against the sea. Dykes, built along the edge of a body of water, prevent water from flooding onto the adjacent lowland. The Zuiderzee Works (North Sea Reclamation Works) in the Netherlands are an immense series of dykes.

COASTS

Dykes were also built to reclaim land from the sea. This reclaimed land requires drainage. Windmills and pumps lift the water off the land into canals and prevent the water table from rising too high.

This endless struggle against the sea has resulted in unique flat, fertile landscapes punctuated by windmills and canals. Wheat, barley, sugar beet and other crops are grown on the new fertile farmlands called 'polders'.

Discussing the photograph

▶ Discuss with the children where the Netherlands is located. Do they know what features the land has (see above)?
▶ Tell the children that the photograph shows a dyke in the Netherlands. Explain what a dyke is (see above).
▶ Explain how and why dykes have been constructed there (either to reclaim land from the sea or to protect low-lying land from being flooded).
▶ Ask the children to identify different features in the photograph.
▶ Discuss with the children the reclamation of land in the Netherlands and how this land is often used (see above).

Activities

▶ In groups, ask the children to plan a route from their home to the Netherlands. Support them by asking questions, such as: Which continent is the Netherlands in? What forms of transport could they use? Would they fly or travel by ferry? Which direction would they travel in? Ask each group to compare their routes. As a class, decide which route would be the best and why.
▶ Read the story of the little Dutch boy who, it is claimed, saved the Netherlands from being flooded by putting his fist in a hole in a dyke. Ask the children to retell the story in a cartoon strip.

USES OF COASTAL AREAS

Bournemouth: busy seaside, Bournemouth: sandy beach

Bournemouth is a seaside resort, on the Purbeck coast in Dorset. It is one of the most popular tourist destinations on the English south coast, because of its fine long, flat, sandy beach, the wide range of accommodation and entertainment, the mild climate and easy access to the Dorset, Hampshire and Devon countrysides.

Before the start of the 19th century, Bournemouth didn't exist. The first settler came to the area in 1810. He bought several acres of land and planted pine trees there. The tree-covered area provided a sheltered walk to the beach, around which the town grew. Bournemouth quickly became a resort for wealthy holiday-makers and for invalids in search of the reviving sea air.

The meadows on either side of the Bourne stream were drained in the 1860s and became the town's Central Gardens. Bournemouth's growing popularity led to the development of many features of a typical seaside resort (theatres, concert halls, cinemas and more hotels) and it remains popular today.

'Bournemouth: busy seaside', shows the beach on a warm sunny day in August. The flat sandy beach is full of people, sunbathing, playing, paddling and swimming. Hotels can be seen, located on the cliff tops. 'Bournemouth: sandy beach' shows the clean, sandy beach backed by steep cliffs.

Discussing the photographs

▶ Show the two photographs to the children and explain that these are two views of the beach at Bournemouth. How can they tell that this area is part of a seaside resort rather than an isolated beach? (The safety patrol boat, the hotels, the amount of people.)
▶ Discuss in greater detail what the people are doing in the photographs. Why do the children think people visit areas like this?
▶ Ask the children to describe the photographs as if they are in the scenes. What can they see, hear, smell? Who might they meet? What sort of activities might they do? Which scene would they prefer to be in?

Activities

▶ Ask the children to find Bournemouth on a map or atlas.

▶ Carry out a class survey to find out which seaside resorts in Britain the children have visited. Make a class chart or block graph of the results. Which resorts have been visited the most often? Are these the resorts nearest to the home area?

▶ In pairs, ask the children to use maps and make lists of coastal settlements which have 'mouth', 'bay', 'quay' or 'port' in their name. Ask the children to make a graph of their results. Which of these is used most often in the names of coastal settlements?

▶ 'Bournemouth: sandy beach' shows a safety boat in the foreground. Explain to the children that some people live and work at the seaside, and make a class list of different jobs people do there.

Video: Aerial beach scene

Zandvoort in the Netherlands is one of Holland's most popular resorts, as it is only about 30 minutes' drive from Amsterdam. The wide sandy beach is enjoyed by families, as seen in the short video clip.

Video: Windsurfing

Windsurfing has become increasingly popular over the last 30 years, particularly with young adults, as it combines the thrills of surfing with the tranquility of sailing. Windsurfing takes place on lakes and rivers, as well as in the sea. In colder waters, it is necessary to wear a wetsuit, and to make sure the water and weather conditions are safe.

Discussing the videos

▶ Explain to the children that the two video clips show people using coastal areas for pleasure. The 'Aerial beach scene' shows people enjoying activities including sunbathing, paddling, building sandcastles on a beach in the Netherlands. Ask the children what other activities and features they can see in the video clip.

▶ Ask the children to look carefully at the 'Windsurfing' video. What is the windsurfer wearing? Also encourage them to talk about his surfboard and sail.

▶ Discuss with the children other activities enjoyed by people visiting the coast (sailing, swimming).

Activities

▶ After showing the children the videos, ask them, in pairs, to list as many different ways people can enjoy themselves on beaches. Ask them to mime some of the activities for other children to guess what they are doing.

▶ Let the children draw cartoons to represent the following activities: paddling, swimming, sailing, kite flying, building sandcastles, sunbathing.

▶ Ask the children to discuss the similarities and differences between the 'Aerial beach scene' video and the 'Bournemouth: busy seaside' photograph (provided on the CD).

▶ In groups, ask the children to name some of the human features found in seaside resorts (fun fairs, piers, museums). Ask the groups to compare and contrast buildings and human features found in a seaside resort with those found in the local area, and to list these. Can they make a list of human features found both at the seaside and in the local area?

▶ Ask the children, in groups, to consider the statement 'Coastal area under threat' for the following groups of people: hotel owners, residents, conservationists, tourists, retired people. Ask them to discuss how coasts should be managed for the benefit of each of these groups of people, while at the same time ensuring developments are sustainable and not damaging to the coast.

Ferry terminal at Dover

Dover is situated at England's closest point to France and the rest of mainland Europe. The Old English name for Dover was 'dubra' meaning 'the waters'. Dover is Britain's busiest passenger port and the busiest ferry port in northern Europe. From Dover, vessels sail to Boulogne, Calais and Dunkerque in France. Dover has excellent communication with London and the rest of Britain, via road and rail links.

COASTS

Roll-on/roll-off ferries, high-speed catamarans, and bulk cargo and container ships operate from Dover. Each type of ship has its own harbour buildings and equipment. This photograph shows the Hoverspeed terminal at Dover. In the foreground you can see the terminal buildings and in the background a 'Superseacat' is docked alongside the harbour wall.

Discussing the photograph
▶ Ask the children what they think this photograph shows and then tell them the details (see above). Can they see the name of the ferry?
▶ Explain to the children that roll-on/roll-off ferries are ships with large doors at the bow (front) and stern (back). Point out the bow doors that are open in the photograph.
▶ Point out the light beacon at the end of the harbour wall, used to guide vessels into the harbour. Why do the children think this is a crucial feature on a coastline?

Activities
▶ Ask the children to use a map or an atlas to work out a route from their home to Dover. Ask questions, such as: How far is it? How long will it take? Which roads and motorways would you travel on? Which towns and cities would you pass through?
▶ In pairs, ask the children to discuss why Dover is in a good position for a port.
▶ In groups, ask the children to use reference books and the internet to find out how many passengers, cars, coaches and lorries pass through Dover each year.
▶ Ask the children, in groups, to find out how the area around Dover and the coast is being damaged by the amount of traffic and heavy lorries using the port.

Fleetwood fishing port

This photograph shows Jubilee Quay in Fleetwood, Lancashire. In the foreground are trawlers and fishing boats, and in the background are containers. There is a freight and passenger ferry service from here to Larne in Northern Ireland.

Fleetwood was once a famous fishing port, with a thriving seafood industry. In 1876 the amount of shellfish and fish being shipped from the town was 100 tons a day, and by 1893 the port had 95 sailing vessels based there.

In 1892, the opening of Preston Dock, followed two years later by the Manchester Ship Canal, had a large impact on Fleetwood. The construction of the canal meant that the cargoes of sugar, flax and timber no longer had to be transferred to trains at Fleetwood; they could now be unloaded at Manchester, the North-West's industrial heart, thereby reducing transport costs. Although the First World War disrupted fishing operations, the port reached its peak in the 1930s. However, the fishing industry in Fleetwood declined from the 1960s onwards. In more recent years, EEC fishing quotas have had a devastating effect on the fishing industry.

Today, people enjoy visiting the jetties, where the small number of Fleetwood trawlers still offload their catch. Many visitors enjoy hiring or chartering the local boats to try their hand at sea angling.

Discussing the photograph
▶ Ask the children to describe what they can see in the foreground and background of the photograph. Explain what the photograph shows, and the history of Fleetwood's fishing industry (see above).
▶ Ask the children to discuss what working on a trawler might be like.
▶ Ask the children to describe the features of the trawlers in detail.

Activities
▶ Give the children maps of the UK and ask them to locate Fleetwood (Lancashire), Preston, Manchester and the Manchester Ship Canal.
▶ Give small groups a copy of the photograph stuck onto a piece of A3 paper. Ask them to list questions they would like to ask. For example, What is it like to work on a trawler? How do fishermen know where the fish are? Are there always plenty of fish in the sea? Why has the port of Fleetwood declined? Use these questions as the basis for the children to undertake some research.
▶ Write the following statement on the board: 'Fleetwood is a thriving seaside resort and busy port, with a traditional pier, a beautiful yacht marina and a promenade full of attractions.' Ask the children to write bullet points agreeing or disagreeing with this statement.

COASTS

Pleasure boats in Poole Harbour

Poole is a popular tourist town and port on the coast of Dorset (on the English Channel), with a population of about 139,000. Poole Harbour is Europe's largest natural harbour. It has been a busy fishing and working port since the 15th century, and was one of England's busiest ports in the 18th century. Transatlantic trade and travel gradually declined in the 19th century because the harbour was too shallow to take the larger modern ships that were being built. They had to use the deepwater ports of Southampton, Plymouth and Liverpool instead. However, Poole played an important part in the D-Day landings during the Second World War because many of the ships departed from here.

Although the harbour has declined as a working port, it is still a point of departure for ferries to France and its quay is a hive of activity, with fishing boats, yachts, powerboats, pleasure cruisers and plenty of waterside attractions. The sheltered and calm harbour is an ideal location for water sports. Yachting is a particularly popular activity.

There is a lot of residential development to the north, but the harbour's western and southern reaches remain a natural complex of mudflats, salt marshes, inlets and reed beds. Four rivers – the Frome, the Piddle, the Corfe and the Sherford – drain into Poole Harbour.

Discussing the photograph
- The photograph shows pleasure cruisers in the harbour at Poole in Dorset.
- Ask the children to describe the boats in the picture. Compare and contrast these boats to those shown in 'Fleetwood fishing port'.
- Explain to the children the history of Poole.

Activities
- Ask the children, using maps of the UK, to locate Poole, Bournemouth and Dorset.
- Give the children reference books, tourist brochures and internet access, and ask them to create a factfile about Poole, listing the tourist attractions.
- Give the children copies of the 'Map of the Purbeck coast' and other photographs in the Resource Gallery that relate to the Purbeck coast and Bournemouth. Ask the children to plan places that holidaymakers who own boats might like to visit.

ENERGY PRODUCTION

Offshore wind farm

Electricity is produced using several different sources of fuel. Most conventional power stations burn fossil fuels (coal, oil or gas) to drive the turbines, or use nuclear reactions. However, burning fossil fuels causes damage to the environment through acid rain (causing water pollution and damage to trees and buildings), and also contributes to the greenhouse effect and global warming (affecting weather, sea currents, farming and water supplies). Stocks of coal, oil and gas are also limited. Nuclear power stations produce radioactive waste, which is extremely dangerous and needs to be stored for centuries before it can be disposed of safely.

Wind is a renewable energy source, which is safe, cheap, sustainable, clean and free of pollution. No harmful emissions are produced when electricity is produced by wind turbines. Sheep and cattle can graze and crops can grow in the same fields where wind turbines are generating electricity. Wind turbines don't need any fuel to be transported to them, nor do they produce any waste which needs to be taken away for disposal. At the end of their useful life they can be taken down and the steel can be recycled.

There are, however, some disadvantages associated with wind power. Wind strength varies from place to place and from season to season, as well as throughout the day. If wind speed drops below a certain level, it is not powerful enough to turn the turbines to generate electricity, so the site and location of wind farms is important. Some have argued that the visual impact of wind turbines (up to 60m high) is a form of 'visual pollution', especially as they cover vast areas. However, careful design and siting (possibly out at sea) aims to minimise sensitive visual impact. The impact on wildlife, particularly birds if the turbines are sited in their migratory flight path, has to be carefully assessed. Other issues include noise pollution and interference that may affect TV and radio communications.

COASTS

This photograph shows an offshore wind farm, consisting of nine wind turbines erected along the East Pier at Blyth Harbour, Northumberland. It is the UK's first semi-offshore wind farm and each turbine is capable of generating 300kW of electricity. The total capacity of the farm is 2.7MW, enough electricity for over 1,500 households.

The wind turbine is connected to a gearbox, which greatly increases the speed of rotation to the generator, making it fast enough to generate electricity.

Discussing the photograph
▶ What can the children see in the background of the photograph? Explain to them where this wind farm is and how much electricity it generates (see above).
▶ Discuss the different ways used to produce electricity from fossil fuels and nuclear fuels.
▶ Explain to the children how electricity is produced from wind turbines.
▶ How big do the children think wind turbines are? Were their suggestions accurate?

Activities
▶ In groups, ask the children to discuss reasons why people may be in favour of or against the construction of wind farms to produce electricity.
▶ Hold a class debate, asking the children to put forward a case either for or against building more wind turbines in other harbour areas.
▶ In small groups, ask the children to find out about the various energy forms used to generate electricity, using reference material such as books and the internet. Let each group focus on one method, such as coal-fired power stations, nuclear power stations, and solar power. Ask each group to produce an information sheet and present their results to the class.

Offshore oil platform

Oil platforms are huge structures, made in a shipyard and towed out to sea. Some have concrete legs that sit on the sea bed. Oil platforms, such as this one in the North Sea, are used to extract crude oil and gas from the bottom of the sea. While the North Sea boasts rich deposits of oil, its stormy waters often make extracting the valuable mineral a hazardous and expensive job. Conditions in the North Sea can be horrendous! Temperatures can fall as low as -40°C, winds can be very strong, resulting in high seas, and the salt water is corrosive.

Exploration in the North Sea developed in the 1960s, and oil was finally struck in 1969. There are now more than fifty oil fields in the North Sea near Britain. Each field has a number of platforms extracting oil. There are also more than twenty gas fields off the Norfolk coast.

There are many diverse jobs, on an oil platform, such as administrators, engineers, scientists, drilling crews, divers and medical staff. Oil platforms are isolated, but the work is well paid.

Discussing the photograph
▶ Explain to the children that the photograph shows an oil platform situated far out in the North Sea. What do they think happens on the oil platform?
▶ What view do the children think they would have from an oil rig? (A vast expanse of sea, other isolated oil platforms and the occasional ship or tanker.)
▶ Ask the children to look carefully at the photograph. What jobs do they think people have on the rig? Where do they think these people live and sleep? What do they think the workers do in their leisure time?

Activities
▶ Locate the North Sea on a map with the class.
▶ Ask the children to find out about the North Sea disaster of 6 July 1988, when the oil platform 'Piper Alpha' caught fire and exploded.
▶ Ask the children to find out about the weather in the North Sea.
▶ In groups, ask the children to discuss why they think oil is important in modern life.

Litter on beaches

There are many ways that beaches can become polluted. For hundreds of years people have supposed that anything they put into the sea will be carried away. Many coastal towns have poured their raw sewage into the sea. This sewage may be washed up on the shore where it spreads germs. Factories have pumped chemical waste into the sea, warm water from power stations has been returned to the sea, and there has been run-off into rivers and seas from the pesticides and fertilizers that farmers have put on their land. Oil may be washed up on the beach, either from oil disasters or from oil tankers flushing out their tanks at sea. Radioactive waste and toxic waste containers from hospitals have been dumped on the seabed. In some countries, there are now strict laws to ensure that chemicals and sewage are made safe before they are put into the sea.

The photograph shows a sandy beach with a large pile of litter. Litter can be dangerous. People can be cut by broken glass. Plastic bags, discarded fishing lines and nets, and plastic loops that hold drinks can kill sea birds, fish and other wildlife. Flotsam may be washed up onto the beach, reflecting how the things we dump at sea are simply carried back.

Discussing the photograph

▶ Discuss with the children the type of pollution that can be seen in the photograph.
▶ Consider how the beach got like this. Ask the children how this problem can be avoided.
▶ Ask the children to identify other sources and types of pollution entering the sea.
▶ Discuss with the children how pollution and litter affect wildlife.
▶ Can the children suggest what could be done to make beaches clean and safe?

Activities

▶ As a class, discuss the main types of water pollution. Categorise these under the headings 'Industrial Pollution', 'Sewage', 'Farming and Rubbish', and make a list on the board.
▶ Ask the children to select one type of pollution from the list and write down ways of reducing or eliminating it (make new laws, educate people, fine people).
▶ Let the children design a poster to increase awareness that the sea is not a limitless dumping ground. Tell them to choose an audience to aim the poster at (holidaymakers, fishermen, factories).

SEA EMPRESS OIL SPILL, 1996

Sea Empress clean-up operation

On 15 February 1996, the *Sea Empress*, bringing North Sea crude oil to Milford Haven, in Pembrokeshire, Wales, ran aground. For a whole week, the ship was buffeted by storm-force gales, hampering rescue work. Tugs and rescue workers tried to free the vessel, but it remained stuck fast on the rock. Oil flooded out in massive quantities. It took the *Sea Empress* eight days to reach Milford Haven port, by which time she had lost 72,000 tonnes of crude oil.

Heavy oil slicks drifted into Milford Haven, and north and south along 100km of the Pembrokeshire coastline. There were major concerns about the quality of the bathing water at the start of the tourist season (tourism being a major contributor to the area's economy). Parts of the coast path were closed for safety reasons during clean-up operations and climbers were advised against using two of the best cliff-climbing areas in Pembrokeshire. It has been suggested that the impact on tourism throughout Pembrokeshire caused a loss of about £2 million in 1996.

A variety of wide-ranging techniques were used in the clean-up operation, including both high-tech and labour-intensive methods. Aircraft at sea sprayed chemical dispersants onto the slicks to help break down the oil into droplets. Specialised vessels recovered oil from the sea surface, and protective booms (floating barriers to contain the oil) were used to protect sensitive areas of the shore where the water conditions were fairly calm.

On shore, a large workforce was employed. Many people pitched in, using rakes and shovels to move oil from the sand or to move oily sand. Mechanical recovery (bulldozers), trenching and beach washing were used on sandy shores, while the rocky areas required chemical dispersants, absorbent scrubbing materials and high-pressure water hoses to shift the oil. The clean-up operation directly involved over 50 vessels, 19 aircraft and 25 organisations, with 1,200 staff (250 of whom were working at sea).

The sustained clean-up effort and natural dispersal eventually restored the aesthetic appeal of the shoreline. By Easter 1996, major bathing beaches were reopened, and water sports had recommenced in many areas by summer. However, fishing continued to be banned for a short while and buried oil reappeared on beaches after storms in the autumn.

COASTS

Discussing the photograph
▶ Discuss with the children what is happening in the photograph. What are the people doing and wearing?
▶ Explain that the photograph shows the onshore clean-up operation following an oil spill, and tell the children the details of the incident (see above).
▶ Ask the children if they know why oil is transported by oil tankers around the coast of the UK? Who was to blame for the oil spill?
▶ Can the children suggest how oil pollution affects wildlife? How does oil pollution affect people? Can oil ever be fully cleaned up?
▶ Discuss with the children the different methods and techniques used for both offshore and onshore clean-up.

Activities
▶ Locate Wales, Pembrokeshire and Milford Haven on a map with the class. Ask the children to write about this disaster and to include a sketch map.
▶ Ask the children to design an experiment, using salty water and cooking oil, to observe what happens when different ways of cleaning up oil are used (mixing and stirring, skimming, adding detergent, soaking the oil up). Ask the children to think carefully about how to make this a fair test, how to observe both what is happening on the surface and under the water, and how to record the results. Do things change over time?
▶ Ask the children to find out about other oil-spill disasters, using the internet.

Rescue operation of oiled birds

Since most oil floats, many seabirds were affected by the oil spill from the *Sea Empress*, as many species spend long periods sitting on the water. The birds' feathers soak up the oil. The feathers lose their insulating properties, destroying the birds' ability to keep warm and preventing them from floating. They can't fly, feed or preen themselves and die of starvation, cold (hypothermia) or shock. Some birds and animals ingest the oil when they clean themselves. This poisons and kills them. Also, if a predator eats an oil-soaked prey, the same result occurs.

Despite a rapid and effective clean-up response at sea, many birds and animals were affected by the oil. The RSPCA set up an emergency bird-cleaning centre near Milford Haven; many other animal welfare organisations ran similar operations. The centre received 3,100 oiled birds of 20 different species. The birds were then taken to local and national cleaning centres when they were fit to travel. Because the Pembrokeshire shoreline was still polluted by the oil, the cleaned birds had to be released at suitable sites near to the treatment centres, such as Liverpool Bay.

The photograph shows an oiled Common Scoter being cleaned and rinsed at a treatment centre. The actual count of oiled Common Scoters totalled 4,700, of which 1,700 received treatment by the RSPCA. There was also concern that for every bird found and treated, many hundreds more may have died undetected out at sea. A total of 6,900 birds were found (either dead or rescued).

Discussing the photograph
▶ Explain to the children that a lot of wildlife was badly affected by the *Sea Empress* oil spill. Ask the children to describe what is happening in the photograph. Why do they think the people have to wear so much protective clothing?
▶ Explain how the oil affected the birds and why they needed to be cleaned.
▶ Tell the children how many Common Scoters were affected and how many could be treated.

Activities
▶ Ask the children to design an experiment using cooking oil and a collection of natural objects (such as feathers and leaves) to observe the effect of oil and what each object is like when it is removed from the oil. Ensure they think about how to make this a fair test.
▶ Ask the children to imagine they are an animal caught up in the oil spill, and to write about how they feel and how the oil affects them.
▶ Ask the children to work out the (approximate or exact) percentage of the birds that were treated in the spill.

NOTES ON THE PHOTOCOPIABLE PAGES

Word cards — PAGE 41-42

These cards show key words that children will encounter when working on this unit:
- words relating to landforms formed by deposition
- words to describe amenities and the types of accommodation found in seaside resorts.

The word cards support the specific study of coasts. Talk the children through the words and ensure they understand their meanings, particularly the 'Deposition word cards'. Encourage the children to build their own wordbank. They could use the word cards to provide captions for displays, and also to help them in talking about the images in the Resource Gallery.

Activities
- Ask the children to illustrate some of the words with diagrams.
- In pairs, ask one child to explain to the other what each of the words means. Take feedback as a whole class, so that any misconceptions can be highlighted and discussed.
- Ask each child to make an illustrated dictionary connected with coasts. The children can add to their dictionary or glossary regularly, as they come across new words.
- In groups, let the children produce an attractive tourist-information leaflet, using as many of the words on the word cards as possible.

Coastal features caused by erosion — PAGE 42

This photocopiable needs to be used in conjunction with the photographs of features formed by erosion in the Resource Gallery. Refer to the notes accompanying each photograph for further information on the features.

Activities
- Ask the children to cut out and match the correct labels to the coastal features.
- Using copies of the photographs in the Resource Gallery, ask the children to match the illustration and labels to the photographs.
- Let the children use maps, atlases and the internet to find illustrated examples of the features on the sheet.

Protecting the coast — PAGE 43

When there is a problem of coastal erosion, there are a number of alternative measures to consider, as sea defences can be both expensive and ugly. This sheet outlines, visually and descriptively, alternative approaches.

The cost and effectiveness of any scheme and its up-keep costs have to be considered alongside the benefits. Also, the effect a scheme has on other areas, what it will look like (its scenic value) and who pays for it are major influences in deciding upon a scheme. In some areas, councils have accepted that they cannot afford to protect the coast. Waveney Council in Suffolk has drawn a line to the north of Southwold, where building is not allowed and no coastal protection will occur.

Activities
- Ask the children to complete the sheet by matching the name and description of the coastal protection to the correct illustration.
- Ask the children to discuss and debate the merits of each form of coastal protection. Make a class list of the advantages and disadvantages of each.
- Give the children reference books and internet access, and ask them to find other examples around the UK of where these methods of coastal protection are being used.

Deposition word cards

COASTS

sand dunes
spit
mud flats
deposit
longshore drift
bar
sandy beach
shingle beach

Seaside resort word cards

COASTS

beach
promenade
pier
amusement
hotel
caravan
camping
bed and breakfast

Coastal features caused by erosion

- This diagram shows examples of coastal features that are caused by erosion.

- Match the correct labels to the coastal features.

headland	arch
bay	stump
stack	cave

Protecting the coast

COASTS

- Match the correct labels to the form of coastal protection.

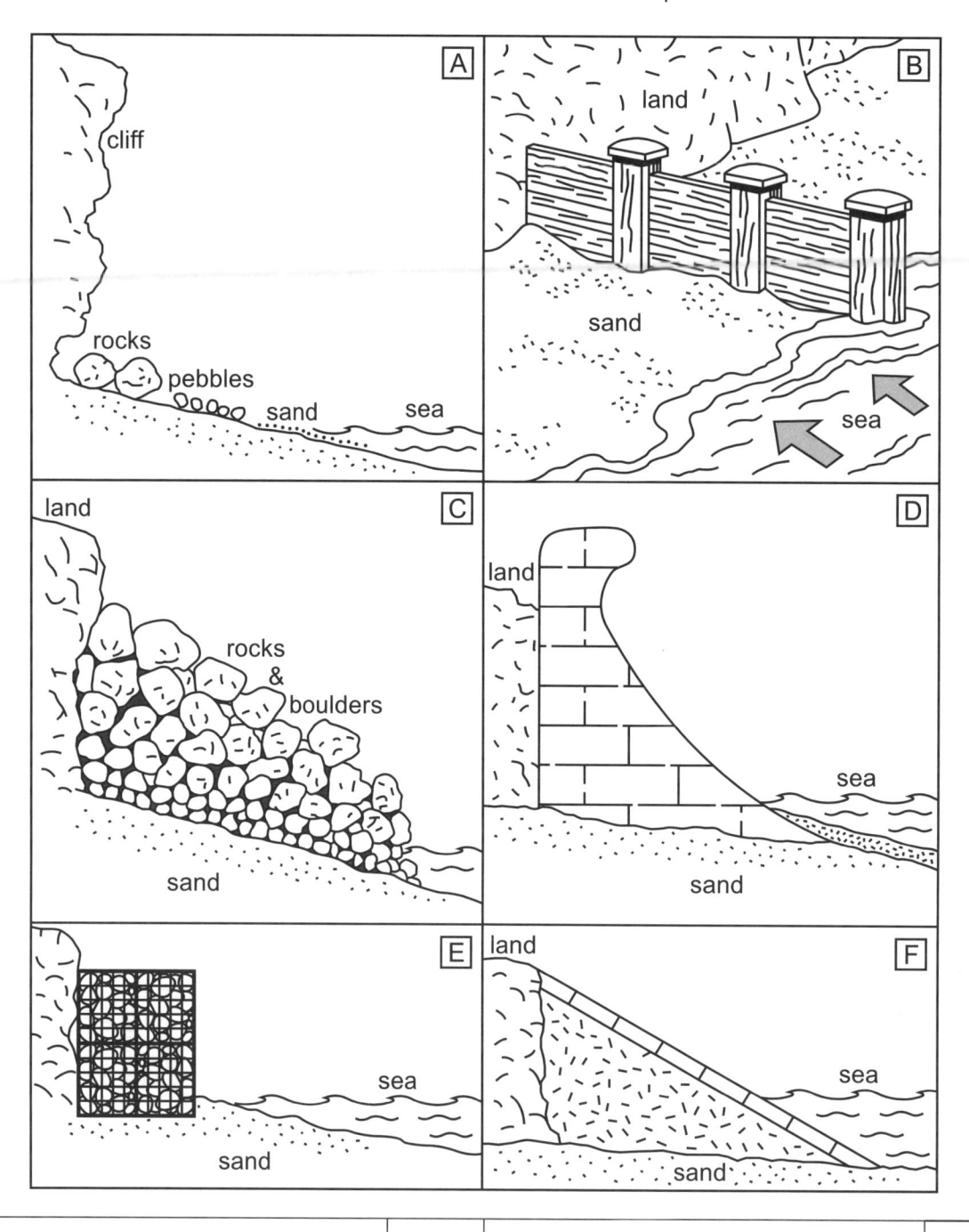

A cliff, rocks, pebbles, sand, sea

B land, sand, sea

C land, rocks & boulders, sand

D land, sea, sand

E sea, sand

F land, sea, sand

Revetment: concrete slope built to break up and absorb the destructive energy of the waves.		**Groyne:** wooden fences built at right angles to shore to prevent sand drifting.	
Do nothing: full force of wave erodes cliff at bottom, creating a 'cliff notch'. Cliff will eventually collapse.		**Gabions:** metal cages of rocks stacked to form a wall and protect cliff.	
Riprap: layers of hard rock with biggest on top. Riprap looks like a natural feature.		**Sea wall:** wall built with curved top and sloping sides to prevent flooding in heavy storms.	

RIVERS

Content and skills
The content in this chapter links to unit 14, 'Investigating rivers' of the QCA Scheme of Work for geography at Key Stage 2. It supports the unit by providing some necessary resources for exploring ideas related to water, and how it affects people and landscapes. The content of this chapter supplements and extends the unit by exploring how rivers play a major part in shaping the landscape. The three processes of erosion, transportation and deposition are investigated, and the effect of these processes in creating features such as waterfalls and deltas.

Through the resources, children are also encouraged to develop an understanding of how rivers can provide opportunities for people, but also cause difficulties. Rivers have always been a major source of water for drinking, transport, industrial use, irrigation, power generation and for waste disposal. Problems that they bring include drought, flood, barriers to communication and, in some hot countries, water-borne diseases.

© Chester City Counil

Resources on the CD-ROM
The CD-ROM provides maps, oblique aerial photographs and ground-level photographs. Through the use of these good-quality secondary resources, alongside independent research using ICT and other resources, the children will develop a good understanding of the close relationship between rivers and people. The resources on the CD reflect a balance of approach, so that an understanding of the physical processes and human development are explored side-by-side.

Photocopiable pages
The photocopiable resources within the book will enable children to develop geographical vocabulary associated with the work of a river, know about different stages in a river's course, recognise and name features on that journey and develop an understanding of how water is used. They are also provided in PDF format on the CD and can be printed out from there. They include:
▶ word cards on the use of water in the developed world
▶ word cards on pollution
▶ a labelling exercise to recognise the features of a river
▶ a matching activity to understand how rivers work.

The teacher's notes that accompany the photocopiable pages include suggestions for developing discussion and using them as whole-class, group or individual activities.

Geographical skills
Skills developed through activities using these resources include map reading and interpretation, identification of key features within visual images and the development of the relevant geographical vocabulary. Geographical enquiry is promoted, and children are encouraged to ask geographical questions, collect and analyse evidence and draw conclusions. The children are encouraged to identify and explain the different views people hold about geographical issues, such as pollution and floods. Knowledge and understanding of places are developed as children locate river systems, describe where the places are, why they are like they are, and how and why places change over time. Children's understanding of how people can improve and manage rivers sustainably or damage our waterways is investigated.

RIVERS

NOTES ON THE CD-ROM RESOURCES

Rivers around the world

The map shows the continents of the world and the major rivers. The world's rivers change and shape the landscape by eroding, transporting and depositing material. Moving water creates all sorts of different types of landscapes, depending on the rock type and the speed of the water. The physical environments, so formed, impact on the way the land may be used, and so on the lives of the people who live there.

Discussing the map
▶ Show the map to the children and ask them to tell you the names of the continents.
▶ Discuss each of the rivers, stating which continent they are in and finding out what the children know about each one.
▶ Discuss the source of each river and the fact that each river flows into a sea or an ocean. Point out that some rivers start in mountainous regions.

Activities
▶ Ask the children to find out, using reference books and the internet, about two non-European rivers. Ask them to sketch a map and to label features on each river's journey (the source, the countries the river flows through, the mouth, the sea or ocean it flows into, tributaries, lakes, important towns and cities).
▶ Get the children to produce factfiles about their selected rivers.
▶ Through questioning and observation, reinforce the concept that water flows downhill. On a rainy day, ask the children to watch what happens to the water. What happens when the rain hits a sloping roof or a slope on the playground?

Rivers in Europe

Hundreds of rivers and their tributaries cross the European continent. This map shows 11 European rivers, all over 1000km long, plus the River Thames. The Volga (3690km) is the longest river in Europe and flows into the Caspian Sea. The next two rivers in order of length are the Danube (2800km) and the Dnieper (2300km), and they flow into the Black Sea.

The River Thames is an important river in the UK. It rises in the Cotswold hills and then flows east across England and through London. Its importance is not so much as a navigable river, but because of the way the river and its tributaries have cut gaps through the surrounding hills.

Discussing the map
▶ Ask the children to look at the map and discuss with them the use of a scale (which can be shown as a proportion, ratio, divided line, ruler or as a written statement) and direction (north is usually at the top of the page).
▶ Are the children able to tell you that the rivers shown are all located in Europe? Explain that they are all over 1000km long.
▶ Discuss which rivers flow into the various stretches of water.
▶ Tell the children that the map also shows the upland areas of Europe. As a class, locate and name the major mountain ranges of Europe.
▶ Ask the children to tell you the rivers that flow north to the sea and those that flow south to the sea. Are there any other rivers which flow in a different direction? Can the children tell you which direction these flow in?
▶ Select a few of the rivers and discuss their source, the countries they flow through and the sea or ocean they flow into.

Activities
▶ Give each child a copy of the map. In pairs, one child can give their partner clues about which river they are thinking of while their partner uses the clues to guess the river.
▶ Ask the children to produce factfiles about their selected rivers.
▶ In groups, ask the children to make up a Snap-type card game, trying to match the names of rivers to their beginning or their end.

RIVERS

Rivers in the British Isles

The map shows the physical features (upland areas, rivers, seas) and countries in the British Isles. From the map, the children will be able to locate major rivers in the British Isles, find the longest river and use the scale to work out its approximate length. They can also see the relationship between mountainous areas and where the rivers start.

Discussing the map
▶ Discuss with the children the use of scales and direction on maps. Can they find the scale and compass on this map?
▶ With the children, locate and name some of the upland areas.
▶ Ask the children to tell you which countries make up the British Isles (United Kingdom and the Republic of Ireland) and which seas surround the British Isles.
▶ Can the children tell you which river is nearest to their own locality?
▶ Explain to the children that rivers flow from high to low ground and generally from an inland, mountainous area towards the coast. Explore the map with the children and find out if all the rivers flow towards the sea. Do they all reach the sea?

Activities
▶ Give each child a copy of the map. Using the scale, ask the children to estimate the length of the rivers.
▶ Ask the children to find out about a river in the local area and draw it onto the map.
▶ Provide the children with an outline map of a local river's course and ask them, using an atlas and other maps, to locate and label features on its journey.
▶ Ask the children to produce a factfile about a local river.

The water cycle

The water cycle is the process (a series of events that cause changes in a place or environment) by which water evaporates from the sea as vapour, condenses to form clouds as the atmosphere cools, and falls again as rain and snow (precipitation). Rivers, lakes, seas and puddles are formed as part of the water cycle. The meltwater from snow and glaciers, as well as surface run-off and groundwater, accumulate and flow seawards from upland areas.

Discussing the diagram.
▶ Tell the children what the diagram shows. Talk through the process of the water cycle.
▶ Ask the children what form the water takes at the different stages of the cycle.
▶ Ask the children what kind of geographic features can be seen at various stages of the cycle (mountains, rivers, lakes).

Activities
▶ Using the other photographic resources on the CD, produce a display to link geographic features to the water cycle.
▶ Ask the children to imagine that they are water droplets. Ask them to draw a cartoon strip to illustrate their journey through the water cycle, reminding them to make a note of geographic features along the way.
▶ Ask the children to write a story of their journey as a water droplet from being frozen in a glacier, to reaching the sea and returning to the mountain as snow.

PHYSICAL FEATURES OF RIVERS

Source of the River Ganges

This photograph shows Gaumukh along the Gangotri glacier, which is 18km from the town of Gangotri. The glacier is the source of the River Ganges and it is high in the mountains of the Himalayas (4000m above sea level). There are many different ways in which rivers can begin:
▶ Some rivers begin as a spring, where water flows out from between the layers of rock.
▶ Some rivers start from small channels called rills, which are formed in upland areas as a result of heavy rainfall.

▶ In other places, rainwater can't sink into the ground as it is already saturated. The water flows out from the marshy ground or bog.
▶ The source of some rivers is a lake. The source of the White Nile is Lake Victoria.
▶ Some rivers, like the Ganges, begin from the water from a melting glacier.

The Ganges flows for 2500km across India into Bangladesh, where it enters the Bay of Bengal and the Indian Ocean. Over 350 million people in India and Bangladesh use the waters of the River Ganges in their homes (for drinking, cleaning and washing), in their factories, on their farms and as a means of transport. Hindus consider the river to be the goddess Ganga. Many make pilgrimages to the river to bathe in the holy water. Others cremate their dead on its banks and put the remains into the river, because they believe the goddess Ganga will take the dead to heaven in this way.

Discussing the photograph
▶ Can the children suggest what the photograph shows? How do they think it is related to the River Ganges?
▶ Discuss the source of the River Ganges with the children and explain how a river can start from a glacier (refer to the 'Mountains' chapter for information on glaciers).
▶ Tell the children where the glacier in the photograph is. They may be surprised that the location is India. Challenge any misconceptions of India's climate and terrain.

Activities
▶ Using the 'Rivers around the world' map (provided on the CD), ask the children to locate the Ganges. Point out where the source is.
▶ Ask the children to locate the River Ganges on a map and trace its route through India and Bangladesh. Ask them, in groups, to discuss the features it passes on its journey (such as tributaries, reservoirs, important towns and cities).
▶ Ask the children to use reference materials to find out more about the Gangotri glacier.

Victoria Falls

This photograph shows Victoria Falls, the world's largest, most spectacular waterfall. It is 1.6km wide, with a maximum drop of 128m. The loud roar of the waterfall can be heard from a distance of about 40km and soon the thick mist of the waterfalls becomes visible. The native people call it 'Mosi-oa-Tunya' which means 'smoke that thunders'. David Livingstone, the British explorer, was the first European to visit the falls in 1855 and named them after Queen Victoria.

Victoria Falls is located on the River Zambezi, which is Africa's fourth largest river system. The Zambezi flows through six countries on its 2700km journey from central Africa, where its source is an insignificant little spring in north-west Zambia. Several dams which harness the power of this river have been built, including the massive Kariba Dam between Zambia and Zimbabwe, and Cabora Bassa Dam in Mozambique.

Waterfalls are usually located in upland areas and are formed where erosion takes place at different rates. They can be formed in several ways:
▶ Cap rock waterfalls occur where a resistant layer of hard rock lies on top of softer rock. The water erodes the softer rock at a faster rate, undercutting the harder rock and allowing the water to plunge into a 'plunge pool' below (Niagara Falls, USA/Canada; Aysgarth Falls, UK).
▶ Waterfalls called 'hanging valleys' are formed where a stream meets another valley, which has been deepened by glaciation (Yosemite Falls, California.)
▶ Waterfalls can also be formed where there has been a fault and the land has been lifted up or dropped (Victoria Falls, Zimbabwe/Zambia).

Discussing the photograph
▶ Explain to the children that the photograph shows Victoria Falls on the River Zambezi, between Zambia and Zimbabwe.
▶ Ask the children to describe what they think they would see and hear if they visited Victoria Falls. How would they feel?
▶ Explain to the children where waterfalls are usually located and the ways in which waterfalls are formed (see above).
▶ Ask the children to share any experiences they have of visiting waterfalls. Explain that not all waterfalls are as spectacular as Victoria Falls.

RIVERS

Activities
▶ Ask the children to locate the River Zambezi on the map of 'Rivers around the world'.
▶ Using maps or atlases, ask the children to locate the River Zambezi and trace its route. Can they find where Victoria Falls are located on the river?
▶ Ask the children to use maps to locate some of the world's most famous waterfalls, for example Niagara Falls (USA/Canada), Angel Falls (Venezuela), Great Falls (Yellowstone River, USA).

Buttermere Valley

This photograph shows the view down Sail Beck of the V-shaped Buttermere Valley in the upland area of the Lake District in Cumbria. A 'beck' is a brook or mountain stream. The interlocking spurs – alternate hills in the valley – are caused by the river flowing around the hills.

In the upland areas, rivers flow very quickly, eroding valley floors through downwards and sideways cutting actions. The resulting feature is a V-shaped valley, so called because it often has very steep sides and narrow valley floors. Further down the river's course, where the gradient isn't so extreme, the valley floor widens and the valley's sides become flatter and less steep.

Discussing the photograph
▶ Tell the children where the photograph was taken and explain the term 'beck'.
▶ Discuss with the children the particular features of this upland river.
▶ Point out to the children that the shape of the valley is like a letter 'V'. Explain how it has formed (see above).
▶ What other factors do the children think influence the shape of a valley? (Gradient, rock-type and climate – the impact of ice, wind, rain.)

Activities
▶ Ask the children to locate Buttermere Valley on a map.
▶ Ask the children to use the photograph to draw a sketch map and to label the features they can see (the upland area, the V-shaped valley, interlocking spurs, steep sides, the narrow valley floor).
▶ Using maps and other reference materials, ask the children to make a model of Sail Beck from source to mouth, and then to give reasons for how the river valley changes its shape along the river's course.
▶ Give the children a copy of 'The work of rivers' on photocopiable page 63, to look further at how rivers erode the landscape.

Confluence of the Rio Negro and River Amazon

This photograph shows where the Rio Negro (a tributary) meets the River Amazon. The place where two rivers join is called the 'confluence', and a 'tributary' is a river or stream that flows into a larger river or lake.

The Rio Negro, meaning 'black river', looks much darker in colour than the River Amazon. The Rio Negro flows entirely through tropical rainforest and the dark colouration is due to the breakdown of plant debris within the forest. Where the acidic, peaty water is very deep, it appears very dark, almost black. Where the water is shallower it is a similar colour to weak tea.

The River Amazon is the world's biggest river in terms of volume of water, carrying 16 per cent of all the river water in the world. It is the second longest river after the Nile. It flows from the Andes to the sea, a total length of 6577km. The Amazon basin is approximately 6 million km^2 in area.

Discussing the photograph
▶ Ask the children to look carefully at the photograph and explain that it shows two rivers. Why do they think the rivers are different colours?
▶ Explain what a 'confluence' is. Explain that not all confluences are as easy to see as this one and most rivers are not different colours.
▶ Introduce, or reinforce, the term 'tributary'.

Activities

▶ Ask the children to locate the Rio Negro on a map and look at the terrain and landscape through which it flows. Then ask them to write an explanation why the Rio Negro is so called. Ensure they have access to reference materials and the internet.

▶ Let the children start to write their own glossary of words connected to rivers. Make sure they include word such as 'tributary', 'confluence', 'source', 'valley'. Remind them to update their glossary regularly.

▶ Give the children 'River from source to sea' on photocopiable page 62 to complete. This will test their understanding of confluence and tributaries.

▶ In groups, ask the children to find out, using maps, reference books and the internet, about the River Nile and its two headstreams, the White Nile and the Blue Nile. Ask them to locate the Nile, the White Nile and the Blue Nile, and to trace their routes through the African continent. What colour is the White Nile? Why? What colour is the Blue Nile? Why? What happens at the confluence of the two rivers?

Meanders on the River Cuckmere

As a river winds its way across the flat floor of a valley, it slows down and starts to swing (or meander) from side to side, forming S-shaped bends (meanders) by erosion. Most erosion normally occurs on the outside bend of a meander, where the water is flowing faster and has further to travel. On the inside bend, the water is more shallow and flows more slowly as it has less distance to travel. Sediment (sand and mud), which becomes too heavy for the river to carry, is deposited here on the inside of the bend. This photograph shows the River Cuckmere in East Sussex, meandering its way across the wide flat valley.

The shape of the meander can change from an S-shape to a narrow-necked loop called an 'oxbow' (named after the shape of the halter used on ox-ploughs). Oxbow lakes often form from these loops, when the river at the narrow neck of the loop erodes back on itself, floods and cuts a new path. Rivers with well-developed systems of meanders and oxbow lakes include the Mississippi River (USA), the River Seine (France), the Indus River (India/Pakistan) and the River Wear (Durham, England).

Discussing the photograph

▶ Explain to the children that the photograph shows the flood plain of the River Cuckmere in East Sussex.

▶ What do they notice about the shape of the river? Point out how it swings from side to side, forming meanders (S-shaped bends).

▶ Explain to the children how meanders are formed (see above).

▶ Explain how, through erosion, meanders may eventually form into oxbow lakes.

Activities

▶ Ask the children to locate the River Cuckmere on a map.

▶ Ask the children to produce a sequence of labelled diagrams to show the formation of an oxbow lake.

▶ Mount copies of the photograph on large sheets of paper and, in groups, ask the children to label the features they can see.

▶ Give the children a copy of 'River from source to sea' on photocopiable page 62, to reinforce their understanding of meanders and oxbow lakes.

▶ Let the children complete 'The work of rivers' on photocopiable page 62, to extend their knowledge of how rivers erode the landscape, and carry and deposit material.

Delta of the River Nile

The River Nile, the longest river in the world, flows from its main source, Lake Victoria, northwards through Uganda, Sudan and Egypt to the Mediterranean Sea, a distance of 6695km. The two main tributaries of the River Nile are the White Nile and the Blue Nile. Lake Victoria is the source of the White Nile and the Blue Nile begins in the Ethiopian Highlands. At the confluence of the two tributaries, north of Khartoum, Sudan, they form the River Nile.

Deltas are formed at the mouths of rivers when a river, which may be carrying large quantities of silt, flows into a large body of calm water. The speed of the water slows down and much of the load carried by the river is dropped. If the coastal current is weak, the

RIVERS

sediment builds up over time into a delta. Deltas can be described as being fan shaped (River Nile, River Rhine) or like a bird's foot (Mississippi River, Mekong River).

At Cairo, the River Nile spreads out to form a fertile, fan-shaped delta, about 250km wide at the seaward base and about 160km from north to south. Seven branches of the Nile once ran through the delta. Today there are two main outlets: the east branch, Damietta (240km long), and the west branch, Rosetta (235km long).

Discussing the photograph

▶ Explain to the children that the mouth of a river is where it flows into another body of water, such as the sea, a lake or a larger waterway. However, point out that not all river mouths are the same.
▶ Explain to the children that the photograph shows an aerial view of the delta of the River Nile. Discuss how a delta is formed (see above).
▶ What shape do the children think the delta in the photograph is?
▶ Ask the children if they can point out the two main outlets of the Nile.

Activities

▶ Ask the children to find out about the River Nile and its impact on the life of the people living along its banks in Egypt. Ask the children to focus on the fan-shaped delta, and how this impacts on settlements and the way of life there.
▶ Ask the children to find out, using maps, atlases and the internet, about the following deltas: Rhine, Mississippi, Po, Ganges, Mekong. Which ones can be described as fan shaped? Which ones can be described as like a bird's foot? Ask the children to sketch the deltas.
▶ Challenge the children to find out about river estuaries, mouths and deltas in the UK.

USE AND MISUSE OF RIVERS

Transporting goods on the River Rhine

The River Rhine is one of the longest (1320km) and busiest rivers in Europe. From its source in the eastern Swiss Alps, the river flows northwards through Germany and the Netherlands into the North Sea. Its main outlet to the sea is Rotterdam, which is also Europe's largest port.

The river is navigable for 800km from the North Sea to Basel in Switzerland. Ocean-going vessels can reach as far as Mannheim. From there, cargo travels by river barges, as the photograph shows, up to Basel. The Mediterranean Sea can be reached via the Rhine-Rhône canal and the Black Sea via the Rhine-Main-Danube canal.

The main cargoes that are carried along the Rhine are coal, coke, grain, timber and iron ore. Heavy industries, such as steelworks and chemical factories, developed along the river because it is easier and cheaper to transport these heavy cargoes by water than across land. The main industrial sites can be found along the Ruhr valley in Germany. Duisburg is the gateway to the valley and it is the world's largest river port. Over the years, the Rhine has become heavily polluted, but great efforts have been made in recent years to clean it up.

Discussing the photograph

▶ Explain to the children that the photograph shows the River Rhine, which flows through the heart of Europe and is the world's busiest waterway. Talk about why the river is so busy, and why it is important for communication, transport and industry.
▶ Focus on the boat in the photograph. How is it different from other boats the children might have seen? Can the children tell what is being transported? Talk about how goods can be transported by sea and by land. Discuss the advantages and disadvantages of both.

Activities

▶ Give the children a copy of the map of 'Rivers in Europe' (provided on the CD) and ask them to locate the River Rhine.
▶ Ask the children, using a map or atlas, to draw a sketch map of the Rhine from source to mouth and to label the following: Switzerland, Germany, Netherlands, France, Lake Constance, Black Forest, River Ruhr, River Moselle, Vosges Mountains, Basle, Cologne, Rotterdam, Strasbourg, Mainz.

▶ The River Rhine is important for tourism. Either ask the children to produce a travel brochure, encouraging people to holiday along the River Rhine, or to write a rap to promote going on a cruise along the river.

Ferry at Dartmouth

Ferries operate where it is either impossible or not cost effective to build a bridge or tunnel to cross rivers. A ferry is a regularly scheduled boat or ship carrying passengers, and now often their vehicles, across a relatively short expanse of water. Today, ferries form an important part of the public transport systems of many waterside cities. In some cities, for example Venice, foot-passenger ferries operate with many stops. This is called a waterbus.

The type of ferry used depends on the length of the crossing, the number of passengers and/or vehicles to be carried and the water conditions. A cable ferry may operate over very short distances. This is where the ferry is propelled and steered by cables connected to each shore. Chain ferries may be used in fast-flowing rivers across short distances. Ships and boats are used where the distance is greater.

This is a photograph of the Dartmouth Castle, a River Link passenger boat and ferry. It is one of the three types of ferries at Dartmouth that carry passengers across the River Dart. The Higher Ferry (once known as the Floating Bridge) is a paddle boat, which runs on two thick steel guide cables. The Lower Ferry is a pontoon, a floating platform, which carries six to eight cars and is pushed to and fro across the River Dart by a small tug.

Dartmouth is at the mouth of the River Dart. Here, the river is always full of activity, with yachts, ferries, fishing boats, tall ships and on occasions, frigates and submarines visiting the Britannia Royal Naval College.

Discussing the photograph

▶ Explain to the children that the photograph shows a passenger ferry boat crossing the River Dart at Dartmouth. Talk about the other two types of ferries operating at Dartmouth.
▶ Ask the children whether they have been on a ferry. Talk about different types of ferries.
▶ Can the children suggest why we have ferries across rivers and why ferries are used instead of bridges or tunnels?

Activities

▶ In pairs, ask the children to list the advantages and disadvantages of living near a river.
▶ In groups, ask the children to look at a map of their area and find places or settlements with names connected to rivers (names beginning or ending in 'port', 'bridge', 'ford' and 'aber').
▶ Let the children use reference books and the internet to find out about other ferries, such as the Mersey Ferry, and other ways of crossing rivers, such as the Mersey tunnel or the bridges across the estuary of the River Severn.

Canoeing on the River Dee

Rivers are used for leisure activities. All sorts of boating activities take place, such as canoeing, rowing and dinghy sailing. Motorboats and pleasure crafts carry people on trips and outings. Many people like walking along the river banks, enjoying the scenery and the peacefulness of the surroundings. Some enjoy watching the wildlife and birds, while others enjoy fishing

This photograph shows young people enjoying canoeing on the River Dee at Chester. The river flows very quickly at this point, providing some interesting water conditions. Other people enjoy walking along the banks of the River Dee, while others take a trip on one of the many pleasure boats. On most fine days, there are artists, displaying and selling their works of art, and at the weekend musicians play in the bandstand.

Discussing the photograph

▶ Ask the children to look at the photograph and to describe what they see.
▶ Talk about what activity is being shown. Explain to the children that the photograph shows young people enjoying canoeing on the River Dee in Chester.
▶ Ask the children to look carefully at how the people in the canoes are dressed. Discuss the equipment and clothing that are used to help keep them safe while they are having fun (helmets, life jackets).

RIVERS

Activities
▶ In pairs, ask the children to think of different ways that people can enjoy themselves on or near rivers. Ask the pairs to mime some of the activities while the rest of the class guess what they are doing.
▶ Ask the children to draw cartoons to represent the following activities, which may be enjoyed on or near rivers: canoeing, white water rafting, bird watching, fishing, rowing, walking.
▶ In pairs, ask the children to design a tourist poster advertising a day out on the River Dee in Chester.

Three Gorges Dam on the River Yangtze

The River Yangtze in China is 6300km in length, making it the third largest river in the world. Its source is high in the snow-capped mountains of western China. The mouth of the Yangtze is at Shanghai where it enters the Yellow Sea.

The Yangzte is an important waterway, transportation highway and commercial thoroughfare for boats and cargo ships. Large, ocean-going ships can navigate up the river for 1000km and steamers can travel as far as Yichang, 1600km from the sea. Shanghai is known as the gateway to the Yangzte and is an important port for cargo ships.

Three Gorges Dam on the River Yangtze is a huge construction project. The enormous dam will have to be earthquake resistant, as it will hold back a reservoir of water hundreds of metres deep and about 400 miles long. The project will enable 10,000 ton freighters to travel easily into the nation's heartland. It will also provide irrigation, flood prevention and will be the world's largest hydroelectric power plant, generating the equivalent electricity of 18 nuclear power plants!

However, there are concerns regarding the project. Some of the major considerations include the high costs of construction, the flooding of towns and villages, and the relocation of about two million people. However, it is claimed that the dam will stop the flooding that killed tens of thousands of people in three major floods in the 20th century.

Discussing the photograph
▶ Look at the photograph of the Three Gorges Dam. What do the children think the large machines are doing? Explain that the building of the dam is a huge construction project.
▶ Talk about where the dam is located and the importance of the River Yangtze.
▶ Can the children suggest why a dam might be needed? Tell them why it is being built.
▶ Discuss with the children why some people are concerned about the building of the dam.

Activities
▶ Divide the children into six groups to represent the following roles: a local peasant farmer, a representative from the construction company, a representative from a local women's group, a government official from Beijing, an environmentalist and an industrialist. Ask each group (in role) to consider how the dam will change their way of life, and whether they want the dam and reservoir to be built. Get each group to list three statements that express their views about the development. Then ask the children to form six new groups, each comprising one representative from the original groupings. In their new groups, still in role, ask the children to give views and discuss their statements, to listen to the views of others and to consider whether their view has changed.
▶ Ask the children, using maps, reference books and the internet, to find out about the construction of the Aswan Dam on the River Nile in the 1960s. Get them to list the benefits and the disadvantages of the dam.

Women washing on the River Ganges, Pilgrims on the River Ganges

The River Ganges flows south-east from the Himalayas, through north-east India to the Bay of Bengal in Bangladesh. Rice, grains, oilseed, sugarcane and cotton are the main crops grown on the vast fertile plain of the River Ganges. Over 350 million people use the waters of the River Ganges in their daily lives. The water from the river is used for irrigating crops, for drinking, cleaning and washing, in the factories and industries, and as a means of transport. The River Ganges also lies at the heart of India's religious beliefs. Hindus consider the river to be the goddess Ganga and that its water is holy. Many pilgrims come to the river to bathe in the holy water, to offer gifts to the goddess and to cremate their dead on its banks. The plain of the River Ganges is one of the world's most densely populated regions and, consequently, the river is also highly polluted. Industries, such as the leather and textile factories located in Kanpur, use the river to dump harmful waste by-products, such as bleach, dye and chemicals. Industrial pollution, added to the human sewage and the remains of bodies cremated on the riverbanks, makes the waters of the River Ganges a real health risk.

These photographs show women washing in the River Ganges and pilgrims on the river.

Discussing the photographs
▶ Ask the children what they can see in the photographs. Discuss how the water from the River Ganges is used for drinking, cleaning and washing.
▶ Explain to the children that the plain of the River Ganges is one of the world's most densely populated regions. Discuss why so many settlements have developed along the river and talk about the consequences of this.
▶ Look at the 'Pilgrims on the Ganges' photograph and explain how the river holds great religious significance to Hindus (see above).
▶ Talk to the children about the problems of pollution in the river caused by the huge mass of population and the concentration of industry.

Activities
▶ Give the children a copy of the map 'Rivers around the World' (provided on the CD) and ask them to locate the Ganges on it.
▶ In pairs, get the children to stick a copy of one of the photographs in the centre of a large piece of paper. Ask them to draw what they imagine is happening around the outside of the photograph, and to draw a picture of themselves and stick that onto the photograph. Can they describe how they feel as part of the scene? Ask questions to prompt them, such as: What can you see, hear and smell? What do you like and dislike? Who might you meet?
▶ In pairs, ask the children, using reference books, to find out about the Goddess Ganga and why the river is named after her. Let the children write Ganga's biography.
▶ Give the children a copy of the 'Use of water word cards' on photocopiable page 60, and ask them to list how they use water (for washing clothes, themselves, cooking equipment) and how this differs from the people in the photographs.

Chemical pollution

Factories are one of the four main sources of river pollution, along with agriculture, mines and people. Today, water pollution is often caused by accidental spillages as there are now strict controls on the quality of the water returned by industries to rivers. Some factories use water from the river and when it is returned to the river it may contain chemicals. Chemicals used in quarrying can seep into the ground water and then into the river. River water is used for cooling, in power stations for example, and it is usually warmer than the river itself when it is returned, which causes changes in the growth rate of fish and vegetation.

Farming can also cause serious water pollution, through either slurry or chemical fertilizers and pesticides accidentally getting into rivers. This photograph shows nitrates from a wheat field entering a river after heavy rain in Leicestershire. Polluted water and rivers carry diseases and poisons that are dangerous or fatal to people and animals when consumed.

Discussing the photograph
▶ Discuss with the children how farming can cause pollution in rivers. Show them the photograph and explain that it shows nitrate run-off from a wheat field.
▶ Discuss with the children how the water would look and smell compared to clean water. Ask them to describe what they think the water in the photograph is like.
▶ Discuss with the children how other activities, such as power generation and quarrying, if they are not managed correctly, may cause water to become polluted.

Activities
▶ As a whole class, list the main types of water pollution. Ask the children to give examples of pollution and categorise the type of pollution under the headings of 'Industrial Pollution', 'Sewage', 'Farming' and 'Rubbish'.

RIVERS

▶ In small groups, ask the children to illustrate a cause of pollution in rivers (oil spillage from a refinery, warm water returned from a power station, domestic sewage from a settlement, pesticides and slurry from a farm). Provide a large-scale drawing of a meandering river to use as a backdrop and use all the children's illustrations to make a class display.
▶ In pairs, ask the children to select a type of water pollution, and to use reference books and the internet to find out how the pollution is caused and what can be done to prevent it. Ask each pair to share the information they have found with the rest of the class.
▶ Give the children a copy of the 'Pollution word cards' on photocopiable page 61, and ask them to link relevant pollution words to the photograph.

Rubbish on rivers

This photograph shows a vast array of rubbish polluting a backwater river in Leicestershire. People can cause pollution through domestic sewage accidentally flowing into rivers. Litter is another form of pollution caused by people. People are sometimes careless and throw rubbish, such as bottles, cans, bags and crisp packets, directly into rivers. Other items of household rubbish, such as old sofas and beds, old fridges, rusty supermarket trolleys and car tyres are sometimes dumped. Not only is it visually unpleasant but the litter pollution has a severe effect on the wildlife in and along the river.

Discussing the picture
▶ Ask the children where they think all the rubbish in the photograph has come from and why it has accumulated here.
▶ What problems do the children think it will cause for the environment and wildlife?
▶ Can the children suggest how these problems could be avoided?
▶ Ask the children if they have seen scenes like this anywhere? How did they feel about it?

Activities
▶ Ask the children to list all the types of rubbish that might be found in a small local stream (empty drinks cans, supermarket trolleys, broken glass, polystyrene and plastic packaging).
▶ Ask the children, in mixed-ability groups, to list six reasons why rubbish and litter in a river is a bad thing. For example, people may cut their feet on broken glass, wild animals may get plastic bags stuck in their throats.
▶ Ask the children to draw and colour a picture of a river scene, which contains ten pieces of rubbish. Ask them to swap drawings with a partner and ask them to identify the rubbish.
▶ Get each child to write a letter (in the role of a concerned member of the community) to the Editor of a newspaper, telling them about the problem of rubbish and pollution in the local river and explaining why the rubbish can be dangerous. Make a class newspaper, adding the pictures from the activity above.
▶ If a visit to a local stream or river can be organised, ask the children to design a data-collection sheet to survey the litter and rubbish there. (NB: You must undertake a full risk assessment, following guidance from the LEA and/or DfES, and all health and safety precautions must be taken.) Ask the children to use ICT (such as a spreadsheet) to record and analyse the data.
▶ Using the 'Pollution word cards' on photocopiable page 61, ask the children to identify appropriate types of pollution to match the photograph.

FLOODING AND DISASTERS

Flooding at Bewdley 1998

The River Severn is the longest British river (354km long). As the river flows through the West Midlands it gets wider and deeper, and the valley becomes flatter. At its mouth, the Severn forms an estuary and flows into the Bristol Channel and then into the Atlantic Ocean. Associated with the lower parts of the Severn is the curious tidal phenomenon, known as the 'Severn bore'. The river's estuary has the second largest tidal range in the world, about 15m, and at certain times the combinations of the tides funnel the rising water up the estuary into a wave that travels rapidly upstream against the river current.

The Severn is prone to flooding in the winter months. On the weekend of 31 October 1998, many towns and villages along the River Severn were badly flooded. The floods were the worst to hit the area for 100 years. At Bewdley, the River Severn peaked at about 6.4m and was flowing at 455,000 litres a second, which was nearly 10 times its normal level for the time of year. The flooding in Bewdley is shown in the photograph.

The causes of the floods in the Severn Valley in 1998 include:
▶ Building houses, factories and roads on flood plains. This increases the rate of surface run-off and decreases the saturation levels of the ground. In 1998, the speed at which the water reached the River Severn was too fast for the river to handle. The river filled up rapidly, overflowing its banks onto the flood plain.
▶ The ground becoming saturated more quickly as urban areas have a reduced amount of vegetation.
▶ Huge amounts of rainfall, with record amounts falling in October 1998. This rain fell on the already saturated ground, so the run off was rapid.
▶ The flat and low-lying nature of the landscape surrounding the Severn meant that as the water breached the banks it just spread across the land.

The floods caused major disruption to people's lives. As ground floors of homes were flooded with polluted water, many people became trapped or stranded on the top floor of their houses and had to be rescued. Roads and rail services were disrupted. In rural areas, farmers had to move cattle to higher ground. Many councils set up emergency shelters in schools and community centres. The total damage bill exceeded £100 million.

Discussing the photograph
▶ Explain to the children that the photograph is of Bewdley, a 'picture postcard' town and a tourist centre situated on the banks of the River Severn in Worcestershire.
▶ What do the children think has happened in Bewdley in the photograph? Tell them about the severe flooding in 1998 and discuss the causes of the flood.
▶ Can the children tell how high the water levels are in the photograph? Consider the effects on the buildings and on the people who live in them.
▶ Ask the children if they know of anywhere else that has been affected by severe flooding.

Activities
▶ Locate Bewdley on a map. Ask the children to draw a sketch map of the River Severn from source to mouth, labelling tributaries, settlements and structures. Remind the children to use a clear, simple key.
▶ Give groups of children copies of the photograph glued into the middle of an A3 sheet. Ask the children to write around the photograph the reasons why the River Severn flooded Bewdley in 1998 and the effects the flood had on people. Ask them to put a green circle around physical causes, a red circle around man-made causes and a blue circle around effects.
▶ Ask the children to write an account for a local newspaper about the floods in Bewdley.

Flood barriers at Bewdley 2004

Bewdley was one of the towns most severely hit by the floods of autumn 1998 and autumn 2000. In 2000, the water levels were 5.6m above summer levels and the town was extensively flooded three times in the space of six weeks. Records showed that some properties had been flooded at least 50 times in the last 100 years.

Following the flooding in 2000, it was decided to develop a flood management strategy for the River Severn. 'Demountable' barriers, like ones used in Germany, were installed. These barriers are erected when high water is forecast. They were put to the test on New Year's Day 2003 and the photograph shows the barriers in use in February 2004.

Other short-term flood-management measures that can be used, include:
▶ accurate long-range weather forecasts
▶ prompt flood warnings and advice
▶ emergency teams, local authorities and local people working together.

Other long term flood management measures that can be used, include:
▶ tighter controls on building on flood plain land
▶ afforestation (replanting trees back).

Discussing the photograph
▶ Ask the children to describe the river shown in the photograph. How high is it?
▶ Can they see what has been put in front of the houses? What do they think these are? Explain about the demountable barriers.
▶ What features of the demountable barriers can the children see? How do they think the barriers work?
▶ Discuss other flood-management measures that can be used.

Activities
▶ Set up a debate, and encourage the children to discuss the advantages and disadvantages of the different flood-management measures.
▶ In mixed-ability groups, get the children to design an information leaflet giving some instructions about what to do in the event of a flood. Ask the children to think about how people obtain information about floods (TV, radio, Floodline 0845 988 1188), for example moving the elderly and pets to safety, using sandbags, turning off gas and electricity, and what not to do (walk, drive or swim through floods). Remind the children to use numbers and bullets to sequence actions, to use imperative verbs (listen, put, do, don't) and to use words with precision and clarity.

Floods in Mozambique 2000

Over recent years, devastating floods have hit Mozambique. These have killed hundreds of people, and left hundreds of thousands homeless and short of food.

Floods and their effects in this area result from a combination of several factors, including erratic weather, inappropriate building practices (weak and poorly constructed dams and flood protection), people living too close to the river on the banks and on floodplains, inappropriate farming practices, floodgates on dams being opened to relieve flood pressures, the lack of a strategy for the whole of the river basin.

During the floods in 2000, the rivers of southern Mozambique (River Zambezi, River Save, River Limpopo and River Incomati) burst their banks. Cyclone Eline brought more rain to lands that were already waterlogged from over two weeks of storms.

In February 2000, 1163mm of rain fell compared with the average of 177mm. The floodgates on the Kariba Dam on the River Zambezi in Zambia were opened to relieve pressure, sending billions of gallons of water downstream into Mozambique. The floodwaters swept away homes, destroyed crops, wrecked roads and bridges, and destroyed dams. Whole villages and towns disappeared.

The photograph shows victims stranded on the rooftop of a building, waiting to be rescued by the helicopter.

Discussing the photograph
▶ Ask the children what they can see in the photograph. What do they think is happening?
▶ Tell the children that this photograph shows the terrible effects of floods in Mozambique in 2000.
▶ Explain to the children how the flood happened and what caused it.
▶ Talk about the devastation caused by the flood and how it affected hundreds of people.

Activities
▶ In pairs, using atlases and globes, ask the children to locate Mozambique, and draw a simple sketch map, showing the main rivers and settlements.
▶ Mount copies of the photograph on large sheets of paper. Ask the children, in pairs, to list the causes and effects of the floods in Mozambique.
▶ In mixed-ability groups, ask the children to prepare a broadcast for a children's news programme on the floods in Mozambique and their effects. Record their programmes on video or cassette tapes and share these with the class.
▶ Discuss with the children the difference between 'short term emergency relief aid' and 'long term development aid'. Write a list of examples of types of aid on the board (tents, providing seeds for crops, helicopter rescue, building a dam, setting up a refugee camp, vaccinating a child, providing medicines, training a doctor, giving out food parcels, training teachers/engineers). Ask the children to sort and categorise the types of aid under the titles 'short-term aid' and 'long-term aid'.

RIVERS

Floods in Prague 2002

In August 2002, Prague experienced the worst floods in 200 years. About 50,000 Prague residents were evacuated. Aid workers supplied food and fresh water to those forced to flee their homes. The swollen River Vltava was about 7.25m above its normal summer levels. Some of the streets were accessible by boat only, while electricity was cut across much of the city. About 400 animals at Prague's zoo were moved to higher ground using cranes, but a 35-year-old Indian elephant called Kadir had to be put down after becoming stranded and a rhinoceros also died.

Discussing the photograph

▶ What can the children see in the photograph? What do they think has happened?
▶ Can the children suggest where the photograph was taken?
▶ What do the children think the people in the foreground are doing?
▶ Ask the class what they think the effects of flooding here would be? Discuss the loss of life, possessions and power caused by flood water, and how everything is contaminated. Point out that even though everywhere is under water, there is no fresh drinking water.

Activities

▶ In pairs, using atlases and globes, ask the children to locate Prague. Which country is Prague in? Can they find the name of the river that flows through Prague?
▶ Give the children copies of the photographs 'Flooding at Bewdley 1998' and 'Floods in Mozambique 2000'. As a class, compare and contrast the causes of the flooding in Mozambique with the floods in Prague and Bewdley.
▶ In groups, ask the children to look at all three photographs of flooding and to write a caption for each photograph to appear in a newspaper. Display the captions with the photographs.
▶ Play Bedrich Smetana's 'Vltava' to the class, which gives a musical account of the journey of the River Vltava from source to mouth. Discuss with the children the musical story and ask them, in groups, to paint the scenes portrayed by the music.

NOTES ON THE PHOTOCOPIABLE PAGES

Use of water word cards   PAGE 60

These word cards show key household uses of water. Over the years, modern plumbing and labour-saving devices, such as washing machines and dish washers, have greatly increased the amount of water used by people in the developed world. The following shows the average amounts of water used in each of the household activities:

▶ bath   80 litres
▶ shower   30 litres
▶ flushing the toilet 9 litres
▶ brushing teeth   1 litre
▶ washing machine   100 litres

Activities

▶ Ask the children to guess which of the activities on the word cards uses the most water, and to cut out and order them.
▶ The children could estimate how much water each of the activities on the words cards uses. More able children could research this, using the internet.
▶ Ask the children to keep a record of how they use water over a week. In groups, ask them to compare their usage and calculate where the most water is used by their group.
▶ Ask the children to use reference materials to find out the average amount of water used when using a dish washer, when washing the car and when watering the garden.

Pollution word cards   PAGE 61

These cards show key words that the children will encounter when looking at pollution of rivers and water. Water is used by many industries (for power generation, cooling, chemical

RIVERS

manufacture, mining and quarrying, paper-making), and for agriculture and leisure. Some activities, if they are not managed correctly, may cause water to become polluted.

Activities
▶ Ask the class to give you examples of how the pollution on the word cards comes about. List these on the board.
▶ Ask the children to collect newspaper articles of accounts of river pollution incidents.
▶ In pairs, ask the children to make a crossword puzzle that contains words related to pollution of rivers and waterways.

River from source to sea   PAGE 62

This photocopiable resource shows a line drawing of a river from its source to the sea, showing the different features along the river's journey. Moving water has energy and this energy wears things down, moves things and carries things along. Rivers have more energy and are faster flowing in the mountainous areas. They slow down as they wind their way across flat plains and make their way to the sea. Different features are formed as a result of the differing amounts of energy a river has. In the upland areas, the main features are steep valley sides, narrow valley floors and waterfalls. In the lower course of the river, before it enters the sea through its estuary, the main features are meanders and oxbow lakes.

Activities
▶ Ask the children to match the labels to the features shown on the diagram. Give them reference books and images from the Resource Gallery if appropriate to support them.
▶ Ask the children to make up their own game of Snap, by drawing each of the features from the photocopiable onto playing-card-sized cards, and writing the name of each feature on other cards. Ask two children to put their complete sets together, and then to shuffle their cards and play Snap with them.
▶ In groups, give the children copies of photographs from the Resource Gallery and a copy of the photocopiable sheet. Ask the groups to match a photograph to a feature on the sheet. Recap how each feature is formed.

The work of rivers   PAGE 63

This photocopiable sheet is divided into two aspects: erosion, the wearing away of the landscape, and transportation, the carrying away of eroded pieces of material.
   The river's erosional powers work in four main ways:
▶ corrasion – erosion caused by the physical impact of rocks on each other
▶ corrosion – erosion by solution (the water dissolves the rock)
▶ hydraulic action, where the sheer force of the water fractures the rock
▶ attrition, where the rocks that are carried along by the river erode and wear away the channel sides and bed.
   Rivers work in four ways to move and transport material:
▶ traction – large particles and boulders are rolled along the bed of the river
▶ saltation – some small pebbles and rocks hop and jump along the riverbed
▶ suspension – small particles are carried along in the water
▶ solution – other rock material may be dissolved by the water.
   Deposition occurs when the river's energy is no longer strong enough to carry its load. The load is then deposited, either as rocks, pebbles or sediment.

Activities
▶ Ask the children to complete the sheet, matching the labels to the diagrams.
▶ Discuss with the class the ways a river erodes the landscape.
▶ Discuss the ways a river carries sediment and rocks along.
▶ Ask the children to create an illustrated glossary of terms associated with the work of a river.

Use of water word cards

RIVERS

bath

shower

flushing the toilet

brushing teeth

washing machine

Pollution word cards

| litter |
| warming of the water |
| acid polluting the river |
| raw sewage |
| old refrigerator and bed mattress |
| slurry |
| oil spillage |

River from source to sea

RIVERS

- Match the label to the correct river feature.

estuary		confluence		tributary		V-shaped valley	
sea		mountains		meander		source	
waterfall		flood plains		mouth		oxbow lake	

The work of rivers

Erosion

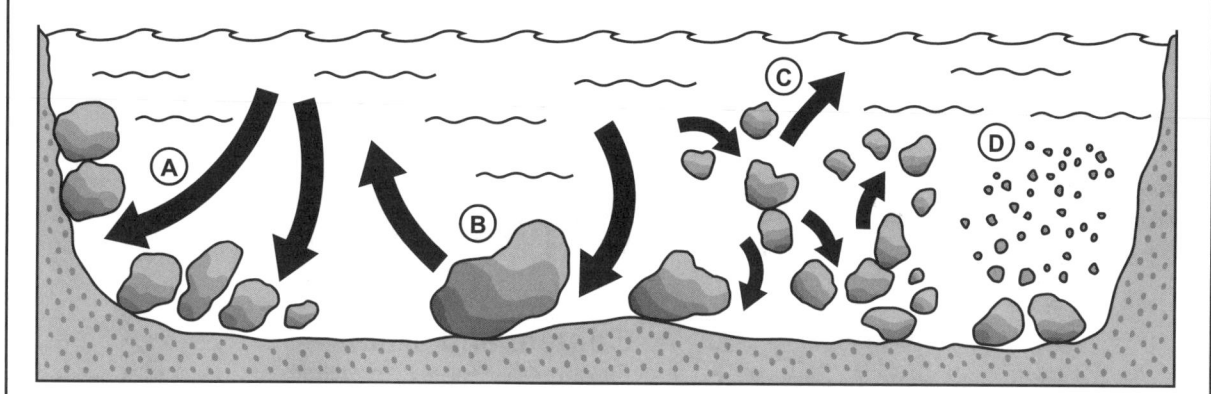

Cross-section of a river channel

- Match the label to the erosional process.

| corrosion | | attrition | | corrasion | | hydraulic action | |

- Match the explanation to the erosional process.

| The force of the water can remove rocks. | Rocks carried along by river can erode and wear away the channel sides and bed. | The water can dissolve some rocks like limestone and chalk. | Rocks and pebbles carried by the river crash into each other and break up into smaller segments. |

Transportation

- Match the label to the way material is carried downstream by a river.

| solution | | saltation | | suspension | | traction | |

- Match the explanation to the way material is carried downstream by a river.

| Larger rocks are rolled along the bed of the river. | Some rocks dissolve in the water and are too small to see. | Some small pebbles and rocks hop and jump along the river bed. | Very small particles are carried along in the water. |

A CONTRASTING UK LOCALITY: PARKGATE

Content and skills
During Key Stage 2, the National Curriculum programmes of study require children to study two localities, one of which has to be a locality in the United Kingdom. Unit 13 of the QCA Scheme of Work offers Llandudno as an example of a contrasting locality in the UK and unit 6 an investigation of the local area. The teaching ideas from these units can be applied to any locality. The content of this chapter offers an alternative example of a locality study. Parkgate is a village in the north-west of England, in the county of Cheshire. The resources in this chapter may be used to provide a good example of how children can conduct a locality study of their own area to compare and contrast with Parkgate.

A sense of what Parkgate is like is developed through the key geographical enquiry questions, focusing particularly on how Parkgate has changed and in what way it is continuing to change. Children are encouraged to investigate and develop an understanding of the influence of environmental conditions on human activities, and how the interaction of physical and human processes brings about change.

Resources on the CD-ROM
The resources include maps that show the location of Parkgate at a variety of scales, to help children develop their awareness of the place within the wider spatial context. An oblique aerial photograph offers a different perspective on viewing the location of a place. The remainder of the resources are ground-level photographs that look at present-day Parkgate, and historic photographs that show how the village has changed over the centuries. Through the use of these good quality secondary resources, alongside independent research using ICT and other resources, the children will develop a good understanding of a different locality to their own. The resources reflect a balance of approach, so that an understanding of the physical processes and human development are explored side by side.

Photocopiable pages
The photocopiable resources within this chapter will enable children to develop geographical vocabulary associated with a locality study of Parkgate. The photocopiables are also provided in PDF format on the CD and can be printed out from there. They include:
▶ word cards relating to the location of Parkgate
▶ word cards to describe settlements
▶ a local folklore story
▶ a sketch map of Parkgate's main street.

The teacher's notes that accompany the photocopiable pages include suggestions for developing discussion and using them as whole-class, group or individual activities.

Geographical skills
Skills developed by activities using the resources include graphicacy, map reading and interpretation, identification of key features in visual images and the development of geographical vocabulary. Geographical enquiry is promoted and children are encouraged to ask geographical questions, collect and analyse the evidence and draw conclusions.

PARKGATE

NOTES ON THE CD-ROM RESOURCES

World map

This small-scale map shows the continents of the world, and locates the position of the United Kingdom to give the children a context of where they are in the world. It also shows the location of the following lines of latitude: the equator, the Arctic Circle, the Antarctic Circle, the Tropic of Cancer and the Tropic of Capricorn. Understanding some of the key lines of latitude will enable the children to appreciate the position of the United Kingdom and Parkgate in the world, and the impact of these locations on climate.

The equator is an imaginary circle, exactly half-way between the North and South Poles. It goes around the middle of the earth for 40,074km, dividing the Northern Hemisphere from the Southern Hemisphere.

Discussing the map
▶ Show the map to the children and ask them to tell you the names of the continents.
▶ Tell the children about the lines of latitude and point them out on the map.
▶ Ask the children to locate Europe on the map and then the United Kingdom.
▶ Discuss the scale of the map with the children. Can they locate the scale on the map?
▶ Explain that maps may be large-scale, showing a lot of detail about a fairly small area, or small-scale, showing a large area but with limited detail. What scale do they think this map is? (A small-scale map showing a large area.)

Activities
▶ Give the children an outline map of the world and ask them to label the continents, the UK, the equator and the lines of latitude.
▶ Ask each child to make a glossary of words connected with the map.

Parkgate in the British Isles

This map shows the location of Parkgate in the British Isles and provides a context for the study of this area. The map also shows the countries of the British Isles and their capital cities. It shows the location of Chester, the county town of Cheshire, where Parkgate is situated.

The British Isles is a geographical term that refers to the two main islands of Great Britain and Ireland, and also includes the many surrounding smaller islands. The two countries of the British Isles are the United Kingdom and the Republic of Ireland. The United Kingdom refers to the United Kingdom of England, Wales, Scotland and Northern Ireland.

Discussing the map
▶ Ask the children if they understand the difference between the British Isles and the United Kingdom. Discuss and eliminate any misconceptions.
▶ Recap the names and location of the parts that make up the United Kingdom, the seas surrounding the United Kingdom, and the name of the capital city of each country.
▶ Explain to the children that the United Kingdom, like many other countries, is split into administrative areas. In England and Wales these are called counties, districts, metropolitan boroughs and unitary authorities. Some 'shire' counties, like Cheshire, are further divided into smaller administrative areas because they are so large, although they still remain part of the bigger county. Each administrative area has its own administrative centre.
▶ Ask the children where Cheshire is located in the United Kingdom. (North-west England.)

Activities
▶ Ask the children to look carefully at the map and to locate the following: the four parts that make up the United Kingdom, Cheshire, The Wirral, Chester, Liverpool, Manchester and Parkgate. They may need to use other maps for reference.
▶ Give the children an outline map of the United Kingdom, with only the country borders marked. Ask them to label England, Wales, Scotland and Northern Ireland, the location and name of the capital city of each country, and where Chester and Parkgate are located.
▶ Ask the children to produce a factfile for each part of the United Kingdom. They could include the capital city, flag, name of the patron saint, main rivers and mountains.

PARKGATE

Wirral peninsula map

This map shows how Parkgate is connected to other settlements on the Wirral, in Cheshire and the north-west of England. The rail network, the main roads and motorway networks to the major conurbations of Chester, Liverpool and Manchester are shown, as are the two Mersey tunnels, Manchester Airport and John Lennon Airport (Liverpool).

Parkgate is situated on a peninsula called The Wirral. A peninsula is a body of land that is almost surrounded by water. The River Mersey is to the east of the Wirral, the River Dee is to the west, and Liverpool Bay (which is part of the Irish Sea) is on the north end of the peninsula.

The name 'Wirral' means 'Myrtle Corner' in Gaelic ('Wyre Heal'). This is because there used to be a lot of forests in the area. In Medieval times, kings and noblemen used to hunt the large numbers of deer and game there. It is thus not surprising that the emblem of the Wirral is a brass-tipped hunting horn that was used by the foresters.

The Wirral used to be in the county of Cheshire until the 1974 boundary reforms. This led to the new county of Merseyside, and the Wirral was established as an administrative area. However, part of the Wirral peninsula, including Parkgate, Neston, Little Neston, Ness and Willaston, remained in Cheshire.

Heavy industry and natural beauty co-exist on the peninsula. The Manchester Ship Canal provides access to the industrial centre of Manchester from the River Mersey, and thus many industries (including General Motors (Vauxhall) and Lever Fabergé) have developed on the eastern shore of the Wirral.

On the western shore, where Parkgate is located, the land is more rural along the River Dee. The marsh of the Dee Estuary attracts a lot of wildlife. Although this side of the Wirral has has little industry now, there used to be a coal mine at Neston that ran beneath the River Dee estuary but it closed in 1927.

Discussing the map

▶ Explain to the children that Parkgate is located within the Wirral peninsula and explain what a peninsula is (see above).
▶ With the children, look for the key and work out what it shows.
▶ Ask the children to look for the compass direction and the scale. Explain to the children how the scale works.
▶ Discuss what the map is showing. Ask the children to look carefully at the main road and motorway systems. Ask them to identify and name the various transport features.
▶ Ask the children to locate Parkgate and discuss its position within the wider road/rail/route context. Make sure they can also locate Cheshire, Liverpool and Manchester.

Activities

▶ In groups, give the children a copy of this map and other maps for reference, and ask them to discuss where Parkgate is in relation to (a) Chester (b) Liverpool (c) Manchester and (d) Birmingham and (e) London and the south.
▶ In groups, ask the children to plan the best route from (a) Parkgate to Chester, (b) Parkgate to Manchester Airport and (c) Parkgate to the M6 to go south to Birmingham. They may need other maps to support this work. Ask them to give reasons for their choice of route(s).
▶ In the same groups, ask the children to describe each of the three routes. They should look for names of roads, towns or villages, physical features and industry passed on the way.
▶ Give the children copies of the 'Parkgate word cards' on photocopiable page 77 to support the use of key words when using this map.

OS map of Parkgate

Parkgate's name derives from Neston Park, which was enclosed about 1250 and served as a deer park for 350 years. By the early 1700s, the number of houses clustered on the banks of the River Dee was large enough to be called a village and so Parkgate was established

During the 1700s, Parkgate was a bustling seaport, mainly due to the Dublin Packet service. Many famous passengers made the sometimes hazardous voyage across the Irish Sea, including John Wesley and the composer Georg Frideric Handel. There was also a daily service to Bagillt and Flint on the Welsh coast. The packet-boat service began to decline in 1810, as Parkgate lost trade to Holyhead due to improved road travel through North Wales.

PARKGATE

Also, the sea journey from Holyhead was shorter, half the time from Parkgate, and also safer and more reliable. So this, combined with the continued silting up of the River Dee and the 'canalisation' of the River Dee on the Welsh side, lead to Parkgate's decline. The last boat to land at Parkgate was in 1811.

Parkgate was a popular seaside resort at the turn of the 19th century, but interest declined as the River Dee began to silt up. However, Parkgate's economy revived when it became a residential and commuter village, with many residents working in Chester, Liverpool and Manchester. Today, the population of Parkgate is about 3,650. The village also now attracts many visitors from the more urban and industrialised areas, who come to walk along the 'promenade', to breathe the fresh air and take in the views.

Discussing the map
▶ Explain to the children that this is an Ordnance Survey map showing the location of Parkgate.
▶ Explain that Ordnance Survey maps use a key to explain what the shapes, lines and colours on the map mean, so that everyone will understand what symbol is used to show roads and buildings for instance. The symbols used on Ordnance Survey maps are called 'conventional' symbols (because they are agreed by convention or agreement by everyone). Point out some symbols to the children, such as those used for churches.
▶ Recap with the children that maps are drawn to different scales, depending how much detail is required. What scale do the children think this map is drawn to? (Large scale maps to show a lot of detail).
▶ Discuss with the children how Parkgate got its name (see above).

Activities
▶ Ask the children to find out what the symbols for the following are on the OS map: church, marsh, motorway, main road, footpath, school, public house. Locate these on the map.
▶ Let the children add new words to their glossary, such as scale, Ordnance Survey, village, marsh. Remind the children to add to their glossary as they come across new words.
▶ In groups, give the children a copy of this map, the 'World map', 'Parkgate in the British Isles' and the 'Wirral peninsula' maps (provided on the CD). Ask the children which of the maps is best for (a) looking at the roads around Parkgate, (b) showing the position of Parkgate in the UK, (c) showing the position of the UK, the Wirral and Parkgate in the world and (d) showing the position of Parkgate on the Wirral.

The River Dee
This is an oblique aerial photograph of Parkgate. Aerial photographs add a significant dimension to locality studies: they make a link between the real world and maps. The features are easier to see and identify in oblique aerial photographs, but there is a distortion because the foreground is in greater detail than the background. In vertical aerial photographs, shapes, sizes and patterns are easier to identify and the photograph can be traced to make a map. Aerial photographs can often contribute additional information that is not evident from maps.

Discussing the photograph
▶ Explain to the children that this is an oblique aerial photograph of Parkgate, showing the view looking north up the Wirral towards Heswall, a larger town.
▶ Talk about how aerial photographs are taken, and discuss the differences between oblique aerial photographs and vertical aerial photographs.
▶ Discuss with the children the purpose of aerial photographs and how useful they are, because they are less abstract than maps and they show what is actually there.
▶ As a whole class, look carefully at the photograph and discuss some of the human and physical features.

Activities
▶ Enlarge the photograph to A3 size and ask the children, in groups, to list the physical features (river, estuary) and human features (houses, settlements, roads, farms) they can see. Tell them they should record the features in two lists or columns. As a whole class, discuss the features each group has collected.
▶ Ask the children, in groups, to discuss and list the reasons why Parkgate is located here

(it's at a crossing point of the Irish Sea, shelter, food, safety). Then ask the children to decide the five most important reasons which made this site a good place to create a village. Ask the children to share these reasons with the rest of the class.
▶ In pairs, ask the children to think about their own locality and discuss how it has changed over time. Ask them to list the reasons for the changes.

TAKING THE AIR AT PARKGATE

Parkgate promenade 1950

The photograph, taken in 1950, shows a high tide at Parkgate. Looking north along the promenade, the sea can be seen lapping at the sea wall. In the 1780s, the area that can be seen jutting out to sea was occupied by a tall narrow building, intended to be a custom house. The building was actually used as an assembly room and then converted in 1812, into warm and cold sea-water baths for invalids. This building, the only one ever to be built on that side of the Parade, was demolished in 1841. In the late 19th century, donkeys used to stand on the area on public holidays, and children could ride on them to the south slip and back for two old pennies. Since this time, this area jutting out into the sea has been known as the Donkey Stand.

Balcony House can also been seen. This 18th-century building, with an iron balcony, was originally the Billiard Room, for men only, but was later used as the Assembly Room.

Discussing the photograph
▶ Explain to the children that the photograph was taken in 1950, looking north along the promenade, and shows high tide at Parkgate. Explain how the use of the area that can be seen jutting out to sea has changed over time (see above).
▶ Point out Balcony House, the 18th-century building with an iron balcony. Again, discuss the change of use of this building.
▶ Ask the children how they know this photograph wasn't taken in 2004 (the clothes the people are wearing, the vehicle).

Activities
See the activities for 'Parkgate promenade 2004', below.

Parkgate promenade 2004

The wide mouth of the River Dee and the calm waters enabled sand and silt to build up and eventually choke the river. Now, the little cottages of Parkgate look out towards the hills and mountains of Wales across marsh grass, instead of sand and the river. Today, you can hardly see the sea. Visitors come to feel the west wind, which blows from the salt marsh, and to look at the stunning views across the River Dee to the Welsh Hills.

The Donkey Stand still juts out, not now into the sea but into the marsh. Donkeys are no longer found there on public holidays, but many visitors sit there, taking in the view and eating Parkgate's home-made ice cream. Balcony House, now painted white, is two homes.

This view looks along the promenade at Parkgate (the road is called the Parade). As the photograph shows, Parkgate is built all on one side of the Parade. There is an old Cheshire saying: 'All on one side – like Parkgate'. The saying signifies the 'raw end of a deal'.

Parkgate has no amusements or tourist attractions. It has a couple of shops selling locally made ice cream, a shop selling shrimps and several restaurants, cafes and pubs. At the far end of the Parade is the Wirral Country Park and the Wirral Way runs through the village.

Discussing the photograph
▶ Explain to the children what the photograph shows.
▶ How can the children tell that this is a modern photograph? (The clothes and cars.)
▶ Point out how the photograph shows nose-to-tail parking along the promenade. Discuss with the children some of the issues that tourists can bring to a small village like Parkgate. Explain that parking is limited and that a traffic calming system has been put in place.
▶ Ask the children how the people are enjoying themselves at Parkgate in the photograph. Explain Parkgate's attractions (see above).

Activities
▶ Ask the children, in groups, to compare and contrast the photograph taken in 2004 with the one taken in 1950. Ask them to focus on how Parkgate has changed and what is still the same. Then ask the children to devise a method of recording what they have found out.
▶ Working in groups, ask the children to consider the pros and cons of tourism in Parkgate from the point of view of different people: day trippers; restaurant, cafe and pub owners; wild life conservationists and bird watchers; ramblers; retired people. Ask the groups to feed back, and then as a class, discuss the requirements of each group of people and how Parkgate should be managed to the benefit of everyone, while at the same time ensuring developments are sustainable.
▶ Let the children produce a poster to show the uniqueness of Parkgate.
▶ In pairs, ask the children to list the impact that people have on an environment like this and how they can change it.

At the seaside 1890
A new type of visitor was attracted to Parkgate as the sands led to the decline of the village as a port for embarkation to Dublin. Throughout the early decades of the 19th century Parkgate was a very popular seaside resort. This photograph, taken in 1890, shows children and families paddling at Parkgate and playing on the sands. Locals continued to bathe here until the 1940s when marsh grass finally took over.

Today, the sands have all disappeared, the waters of the Dee Estuary have disappeared on the Wirral side and the view is of a vast swathe of salt marsh.

Discussing the photograph
▶ Explain to the children when this photograph was taken and what it shows (see above).
▶ What clues tell the children that the photograph was taken in a different century?
▶ Ask the children to suggest what the people in the photograph are doing.
▶ Do the clothes the people are wearing indicate what the weather is like?

Activities
▶ Ask the children to compare and contrast the photograph with 'Parkgate promenade 2004' (provided on the CD). Ask them to focus on how the people in each photograph are dressed and what they are doing.
▶ Using a map and other reference materials, ask the children to find out what the area in the photograph is probably like now. What would be seen from the sea wall in the 'Parkgate promenade 2004' photograph if the sands have all gone?

SHRIMP, MUSSELS AND SHELLFISH

Watching from the slip 1890s
The photograph, taken in the 1890s, shows children standing on the slipway watching a fishing boat. After the decline of Parkgate as a port, fishing became an important industry for many years. From historical sources we know that 13 out of the 235 employed adults living in Parkgate were fishermen in 1841, and by 1871 the number had increased to 25 fishermen.

Loading cockles and mussels 1940s
Parkgate shrimps were a much sought-after delicacy. The railway and the station at Parkgate, built in 1866, opened up the market for Parkgate fish, particularly shrimps and other shellfish. Donkey carts and lorries were used to collect the sacks of cockles and mussels.

This photograph from the 1940s shows small lorries collecting the shellfish, which were then transported to the markets in the industrial towns of the north-west. On Saturdays, a train with 20 to 30 trucks used to leave Parkgate Station bound for the markets of Lancashire and Yorkshire. Sadly, the tradition of shrimping at Parkgate has all but gone.

Discussing the photographs
▶ Ask the children what they think the photographs show.
▶ Ask the children what sort of industry they think the men work in. (Fishing.)

▶ When do they think the photographs were taken? What clues tell them they are old photographs?
▶ Discuss with the children how fishing became an important industry in Parkgate after the decline of Parkgate as a port.
▶ Explain that the slipway was used first by donkey carts and then later, as shown in 'Loading cockles and mussels 1940s', by small lorries, to collect the sacks of shellfish.

Activities
See the activities for 'Shrimp and cockle shop 2004', below.

Shrimp and cockle shop 2004

Today, residents and visitors alike enjoy sampling the fresh shrimps on sale along the Parade. This photograph shows Mealor's shop on the Parade in 2004.

Discussing the photograph
▶ Tell the children what the photograph shows.
▶ When do the children think this photograph was taken? Why?
▶ Ask the children to describe the building in the photograph. Point out how the shop does not have a garden or a wide pavement in front of it, and it opens directly onto the road. Ask the children if they think this would have been a problem when the building was built and why it may be a problem today.

Activities
▶ Ask the children in groups to discuss what life as a fisherman must have been like in the early 1900s.
▶ Ask the children to write a brief account of the fishing industry in Parkgate, including why it developed, where the shrimps and shellfish were sold and how the fishermen got their catch to the markets.
▶ In groups, give the children a copy of the photographs 'Watching from the slips 1890s', 'Loading cockles and mussels 1940s' and 'Shrimp and cockle shop 2004', and ask them to list the changes they note. Tell them to focus on clothes, methods of fishing, vehicles.

THE WIRRAL WAY

Parkgate Station 1906

The railway line from Hooton to Parkgate was opened in 1866 and was extended to West Kirby in 1886. The railway encouraged commuters to settle at Parkgate and brought visitors and day trippers. It also opened up the market for Parkgate fish, particularly shellfish and shrimps. The railway line was closed in 1956 and the track taken up in 1964. In 1969, the 12-mile route was adopted as part of the Wirral Country Park and is known as the Wirral Way.

Discussing the photograph
▶ What do the children think the photograph shows? Tell them about the railway line.
▶ Discuss with the children who used the railway and how this impacted on the development of Parkgate.
▶ Discuss with the children when the photograph was taken. What clues tell them that it was taken a very long time ago?

Activities
See the activities for 'The Wirral Way', below.

The Wirral Way

The Wirral Way, a path on the track of the former railway, is 12 miles long and goes from West Kirby to Hooton. It gives visitors and residents the opportunity to escape the surrounding cities and towns. In addition to the footpath, there is also a bridal way for horses. Horse riding is a popular hobby in the area around Parkgate.

PARKGATE

The Wirral Way is lined with woodland and scrub, and offers cover for many different breeding birds, such as yellowhammers and linnets. Wild flowers attract butterflies, and in the winter thrushes and finches feed on hawthorn berries.

Discussing the photograph
▶ Explain to the children that after the railway at Parkgate was closed the track was taken up and in 1969 the route of the old railway was adapted as a path, which is now known as the Wirral Way.
▶ Discuss how the Wirral Way is an important leisure facility, providing a path, a cycle route and a bridle way. The Wirral Way is also important for wildlife, birds, animals and plants.
▶ Ask the children to identify any features in the photograph that may give clues to the Wirral Way's history, for example, the bridge.

Activities
▶ In pairs, ask the children to list all the ways that the coming of the railway was important to Parkgate and how it helped sustain Parkgate.
▶ Using other reference materials and a map, ask the children to write an account of a journey on the railway from Hooton to West Kirby. Which settlements did their journey take them through? What might they have been able to see?
▶ The Wirral Way has now become an important recreational facility. In pairs, using reference books and the internet, ask the children to produce a publicity leaflet for the Wirral Way.

BY THE RIVER DEE

Boat House restaurant

There has been an inn on the site of the current Boat House restaurant since 1664, when it was simply called the Beer House. It became known as the Ferry House or Boat House when a daily ferry service used to sail from this point to Flint. The inn, later called Pengwern Arms, was pulled down in 1885 after being damaged by storms. The site lay empty until tea rooms were built in 1926, which were enlarged to become the Boat House restaurant in 1977.

Near the Boat House there used to be a large open-air swimming pool. This was opened in 1923 and a children's pool was added in 1930. The Second World War forced the baths to close for five years and then they re-opened only to close permanently in 1950. The site now forms part of the Wirral Country Park and is a vantage point for bird watchers.

Discussing the photograph
▶ Explain to the children what the photograph shows.
▶ Ask the children to notice the advertisements on the restaurant. What does this tell them about when the photograph was taken? (It was taken at the end of November 2004. The restaurant is advertising its Christmas Fayre.)
▶ Explain to the children the history of the site and how there has been an inn on the site of the Boat House since 1664.

Activities
See the activities for 'Birdwatching', below.

Birdwatching

The marsh of the Dee Estuary is of international importance because of the number and variety of birds it attracts. The area is a Site of Special Scientific Interest (SSSI). All the marshland off Parkgate is part of the Gayton Sands RSPB (Royal Society for the Protection of Birds) reserve. Winter waders, such as oystercatchers from Iceland, curlew from Scandinavia, dunlin from Finland, redshank from northern Britain and wildfowl can be seen in the area.

There is a channel that runs past the Boat House restaurant called Boathouse Flash. A variety of birds are attracted to this area; these include warblers and wheatears, finches and greenshanks in the autumn, and little egrets in the winter. The Old Baths car park at Parkgate provides the best vantage point for birdwatching in this area.

Discussing the photograph
▶ Ask the children what they think is happening in the photograph. Explain that there was once a large open-air swimming pool near the Boat House restaurant, and the site now forms part of the Wirral Country Park. The Old Baths car park is a vantage point for birdwatchers.
▶ Tell the children that Parkgate marsh is a SSSI and also part of the Gayton RSPB reserve. Can the children guess what the acronyms stand for?
▶ Are any of the children members of the RSPB? Ask them to tell the other children about their membership and what they do.
▶ Ask the children to name the different pieces of equipment for bird watching that are evident in the photograph. What else might a birdwatcher need?
▶ Why do they think this area would be a good location for birdwatching?

Activities
▶ Ask the children to find out more about SSSIs and the RSPB.
▶ Ask the children to find out more about birdwatching. Are there any RSPB clubs in or near the children's own locality?
▶ Ask the children to debate the reasons for the Parkgate swimming pool being closed.
▶ Using most of the photographs in the Resource Gallery, ask the children, in groups, to create a timeline for Parkgate. The timeline will help the children understand the chronology and how Parkgate has changed over the years.

FAMOUS PEOPLE, STORIES AND FOLKLORE

Watch Tower House

This photograph shows Watch Tower House on the Parade, which overlooks the River Dee. Many early passengers died on the crossing between Ireland and Parkgate, not always by natural means. 'Wrecking' was a common pursuit on this coastline and the wreckers used some quite enterprising methods. One method was to make a donkey lame, and then tie a lantern to the animal's head and make it walk to and fro on the shoreline. From out at sea this would appear to be the mast headlight of a ship riding the swell safely at anchor in the port. The approaching vessel would be beached, or worse, and ready for looting.

Smuggling was also rife. Smugglers and customs officers alike would shoot first and ask questions later. Tea, tobacco and spirits were always top of the smugglers' shopping list. Even the fishermen of old Parkgate may have supplemented their income by this perilous form of employment.

Discussing the photograph
▶ Explain to the children about wrecking and smuggling (see above).
▶ Ask the children to identify the features of the Watch Tower House.
▶ Discuss who used this building and why.

Activities
See the activities for 'Dover Cottage', below.

Dover Cottage

Emma Lyon, the daughter of a blacksmith from Ness, is possibly better known under her later name, Lady Hamilton. Emma Lyon was the nursery maid who became the wife of an ambassador, confidante of a queen. She was painted by Romney and was loved by and the mistress of Lord Nelson. As Lady Hamilton, and often joined by her lover, Lord Nelson, she began frequenting Parkgate to take the air and bathe in the sea. At that time Parkgate had become a very fashionable bathing place. She often bathed in the sea and tried the seaweed treatment in a bid to cure a skin disease from which she suffered.

When she visited Parkgate, Lady Hamilton stayed in Dover Cottage. Next door to Dover Cottage is Nelson Cottage. It was the weekend cottage of Albin Burt, a 19th-century artist from Chester, who admired the great admiral so much that he named his children Nelson and Emma. In 1822, the young Nelson was swept off a ship and drowned. Later, Albin, grieving for his son, set his name in black pebbles outside the cottage. This can still be seen today.

PARKGATE

Discussing the photograph
▶ Explain to the children who Emma Lyon was and why she visited Parkgate.
▶ Point out the cottage where Lady Hamilton stayed in Parkgate and tell the children its name. Discuss why the name Nelson appears in pebbles outside the cottage next to the one where she stayed.
▶ Ask the children to imagine what the cottage was like when Lady Hamilton was there.

Activities
▶ Ask the children to describe in their own words one of the methods used by wreckers to ground ships so that they could loot them.
▶ In groups, ask the children to produce a collage showing wrecking and smuggling.
▶ Using reference books and the internet, get the children to find out about Lord Nelson and to write a biography of his life.
▶ Ask the children to discuss and debate, in groups, what may happen if the sea level, due to the impact of global warming, rose by 20m in the next 50 years. How do they think this would affect Parkgate?

PARKGATE: A CONSERVATION AREA

New houses 1998

Parkgate was awarded conservation area status in 1973, because of its many fine historic buildings. Any new developments are restricted. Over the last few years, there has been some limited development of new houses, particularly on the edge of the village, and the change of use of some buildings. Each planning application is rigorously scrutinised.

These new buildings have been built on the site of the former Parkgate Hotel on the edge of the conservation area. The original building was built in 1862 and was called Richville. The name was then changed to Leighton, when it was run as a school for girls. Finally, the building became the Parkgate Hotel, before it and all its grounds were sold to make way for a modern housing estate. The actual building is still part of the development, having been turned into luxury apartments.

Discussing the photograph
▶ Tell the children about this new housing development (see above).
▶ Explain about the history of the site to the children.
▶ What do the children think of the style of houses in this photograph?

Activities
See the activities for 'New houses 2003', below.

New houses 2003

The new houses in the photograph, built in 2003, are on the site of a former orchard. The development was strictly controlled and limited in number. The architect designed the houses round a cobbled courtyard. All the houses have slate roofs and wooden framed windows. The style is that of old stables, even though the entire development is a new build.

Discussing the photograph
▶ Tell the children that the photograph shows a new housing development in part of the conservation area in Parkgate.
▶ Explain to the children what a conservation area is.
▶ Ask the children what they think of the style of the buildings. Explain how new developments are strictly controlled in Parkgate and why.

Activities
▶ Ask the children to compare and contrast the houses and apartments in these two photographs with some of the other houses found in Parkgate (provided on the CD).
▶ Ask the children, using reference books and the internet, to find out what it means for an area if it is granted conservation area status.

▶ In groups, ask the children to discuss why we need conservation areas. Ask the groups to discuss and debate conservation versus new developments for an expanding population.
▶ In groups, give the children copies of all the photographs and maps of Parkgate in the Resource Gallery. Ask them to identify the features (physical and human) which characterise Parkgate and make the village what it is today. Ask them to consider how the physical and human changes are interrelated.

THE PARADE

Ice cream shop, The Marsh Cat restaurant, The Red Lion, Old Quay Inn

Many of Parkgate's buildings were originally built for purely functional purposes. It was during the 19th century that bay windows were added to the houses. The black and white decorations were added in the 20th century. Today, along the Parade are a small selection of shops, a newsagent, ice-cream parlours, a general store and Post Office, and a wide range of eateries, including pubs, restaurants and cafes. For larger shops and supermarkets, residents have to go to either the towns of Neston or Heswall, and for bigger items to either the cities of Chester or Liverpool, or an out-of-town shopping centre.

Parkgate is famous for its home-made ice cream. The ice cream parlour is also the post office, and sells cards and souvenirs as well. The building in which the ice cream shop and post office are located was built in 1935, following the demolition of an old house. A visit to the famous ice-cream shop is a must for visitors and residents alike.

There are numerous eateries on the promenade, including the Marsh Cat restaurant, established in 1997. The Marsh Cat has wonderful views overlooking the marsh and also has the reputation as one of the best restaurants on the Wirral. The Old Quay Inn was built in 1963, and is on the site of the former Chester Hotel, which has been an inn since 1850. The Customs House, abandoned by The Customs in 1830, was also on the same site.

Other restaurants include Mr Chow's, the Ship, the Boat House and the Red Lion. The Red Lion, which is believed to be nearly 400 years old, is the oldest of the surviving Parkgate public houses to have remained unchanged.

Discussing the photographs
▶ Show this set of photographs to the children and explain that these buildings are all situated along the Parade.
▶ Tell them the brief history of each building in turn (see above).
▶ Ask the children to note the similarities and differences between the buildings.
▶ Can the children imagine what the whole of the Parade looks like if this is just a selection of the buildings built on it? Ask for suggestions.
▶ Discuss who might work in these buildings. What jobs might there be in Parkgate?

Activities
▶ Read the story 'The Marsh Cat' on photocopiable page 79 to the children.
▶ In groups, give the children a copy of all the photographs and maps in the Resource Gallery, and a shoebox. Ask the children to discuss what items they would include in the shoebox to represent what life in Parkgate is like (a map, photographs, sand, a pair of binoculars, a list of birds). They can draw items that they may not have. Then give the groups another shoebox and ask them to put into it items to represent what their own locality is like (postcards, images of local buildings, items made in local industries, map of the UK with the school location marked). This activity focuses on the geographical enquiry questions: What is Parkgate like? How is this place different from my own locality?

FACILITIES AND AMENITIES

Parkgate Primary School

Mostyn Square, halfway along the Parade, is named after the Mostyn Family, who owned the entire village of Parkgate from 1672 to 1849. The road running uphill from Mostyn Square passes the church and the old infant school, now a residential property. The new primary

PARKGATE

school is a modern building, further up the hill. About 170 pupils, both boys and girls, attend Parkgate Primary School. At the age of 11, children leave the primary school and may go to one of several secondary schools serving the area. The nearest secondary school is Neston High School.

Mostyn House Independent School

Over the years, several of the buildings in Parkgate have been schools. Mostyn House, facing the marshes at the southern end of the promenade, is an independent school for boys and girls between the ages of 4 and 18. Mostyn House was originally the George Inn, first recorded in the 1700s. When the Packet Service to Dublin was in decline, the old inn was refurbished and re-opened as the Mostyn Arms Hotel. In 1855, when Parkgate was in decline because its fame as a bathing resort was over, the hotel could no longer continue and was sold off. It was bought by the Grenfell family, who extended it and then opened it as a preparatory school, initially for boys only, but now for both boys and girls. The black and white facade dates from 1932.

Garden centre

There is a garden centre in Parkgate and more in the neighbouring area, serving the needs of the many people who find gardening a relaxing leisure activity. People who may once have farmed the land have turned to horticulture and the selling of plants and gardening equipment as a more profitable way of earning a living.

Pony Sanctuary

Parkgate is surrounded by farmland. Horse riding is a very popular pastime and there are a large number of horses on the Wirral. Some children have their own ponies, which they stable and graze on land rented from local farmers. Other children regularly go to riding centres for lessons. The Pony Sanctuary in Parkgate is a charity which cares for horses and ponies which have sadly been neglected.

Discussing the photographs
▶ Show this set of photographs to the children and explain that these facilities and buildings are all located in Parkgate. Tell them the brief history behind each photograph and the buildings associated with them where appropriate (see above).
▶ Ask the children to note the similarities and differences between these facilities and buildings and similar places in their own locality.

Activities
▶ In the same groups, ask the children to consider if any areas or buildings may not be suitable for small children and/or disabled people.
▶ In pairs, ask the children to list three physical and three human features they would never find in Parkgate.
▶ Working in groups, ask the children to discuss and list the advantages and disadvantages of living in Parkgate from the points of view of: a 10-year-old child, a family with young children, an elderly couple, a couple in their mid-30s without any children.
▶ Ask the children to list three things they would see in Parkgate but not in their own locality, three things they would see in their own locality but not in Parkgate, and three things they would see in both Parkgate and their own locality.

NOTES ON THE PHOTOCOPIABLE PAGES

Word cards   PAGE 77-78

These cards contain some of the basic and more advanced vocabulary for the children to learn and use when teaching this unit. They include:
▶ words relating to the location of Parkgate
▶ words to describe settlements.

The word cards support the study of localities generally and the locality of Parkgate specifically. Encourage the children to build their own word bank. They could use the word cards to provide captions for the resources in this gallery or for displays, to help them in talking about the pictures or to help them with longer pieces of writing. Read through the word cards with the children to familiarise them with the key words of the unit. Through questioning and discussion, develop the children's knowledge and understanding of the terms. Eliminate any misconceptions.

Activities
▶ In pairs, ask one child to explain to the other child what each of the words means.
▶ Ask the children to begin a glossary with these words. Ask each child to explain the words carefully.
▶ Laminate the word cards to use in games with the children. Shuffle sets of word cards and spread them out on groups of children's tables. Ask the children to find specific words you call out.
▶ Using the 'Locality study word cards', ask the children in pairs to categorise the words into those that apply to Parkgate today, those that apply to Parkgate in the past, those that apply to Parkgate in both the past and present and those that do not refer to Parkgate at all. Discuss the use of a Venn diagram to show this information.

The Marsh Cat PAGE 79

The text is a piece of fiction that builds on the unique history of Parkgate. The passage gives some insight into the lives and the perilous nature of the work of the men who sailed the ships in the 1700s. It is also a good example of how local industries, for example the hospitality trade, are building on the uniqueness of Parkgate's past as well as its present.

Discussing the text
▶ Read the story to the children. Explain any difficult vocabulary and sentence structure so they can appreciate the extract.
▶ Discuss whether the children think this extract is fact or fiction. Do they think there are elements of fact in the story? How can they find out? Which bits do they think are fictitious? Why?
▶ Ask the children if they would have liked to be a sailor in 1700s, or the ship's cat.

Activities
▶ Give each child a copy of the text. Ask them to look for nouns and to underline them in red, and to look for proper nouns and to circle the capital letters in blue. Differentiate the text for different ability groups of children.
▶ Give each child a copy of the text and ask them to underline, in green, all the geographical words. Ask the children to add these words to their glossary of terms, or to a word wall of geographical vocabulary and terms.
▶ After reading the story to the children, get each of them to retell it in groups. Discuss the similarities and differences in the retellings. Explain that when stories are retold orally, they are likely to be different because different people will tell them in different ways.

Parkgate Parade PAGE 80

The sketch map shows Parkgate, the marshes of the Dee estuary and the mile-long Parade. It indicates the location of some of the photographs found in the Resource Gallery.

Activities
▶ Enlarge the map and use it as the base for a classroom wall display.
▶ With the children, discuss each of the photographs found in the Resource Gallery. Ask the children to look at each photograph carefully and locate its position on the map. Stick a copy of each photograph on the map.
▶ Ask the children to write about a walk along the Parade at Parkgate.

Parkgate word cards

United Kingdom
Great Britain
peninsula
Cheshire
The Wirral
North-West
conservation area

Locality study word cards

settlement	port
village	urban
residential	rural
industrial	town
seaside resort	city

Story of the Marsh Cat

To the west of Liverpool and the east of Wales, beside the ever-changing sands of the River Dee lies the port of Parkgate. Our story begins in the year 1775 when Parkgate was a thriving port with many ships carrying passengers and valuable cargo around the globe. These ships would often be at sea for many months so the captain would take on board a cat to keep the rodent population down. Our cat was the 'best in the business' and his success made him in great demand. During his voyages he sailed to the Americas, Europe, Asia, Australia and the Caribbean. His job was a very important one and he was often rewarded with food from the captain's table, this being the best food from around the world.

After many exciting voyages and ports of call, our cat was getting old and he decided he wanted an easier life. He had been through too many storms and cruel seas. His nine lives were nearly all used. He decided to retire and was to live with Captain Samuel Davies, master of the ship *Nonpareil*, and his wife, at the Kings Arms in Parkgate.

Our cat had one more journey to make with his master. They were to take Major Castlefield and other passengers, including 43 vagrants from the Neston House of Correction over to Ireland. A routine trip, or so they thought. The weather was bad, even the Captain had a bad feeling about it. They made two attempts to cast off and eventually, under duress, the *Nonpareil* set sail out of Parkgate. This was the last ever sighting of the ship. The *Nonpareil* was sunk in a terrible storm just off Hoyle Bank, no souls were saved.

Legend has it that the spirit of our cat still lives on the marsh in Parkgate; his ghost wanders the parade looking for the best food its restaurants have to offer. His favourite is his namesake, 'The Marsh Cat', this is where he tastes all the delicious food that reminds him of his adventures a long time ago, before the Dee gave Parkgate to the marsh.

Parkgate promenade

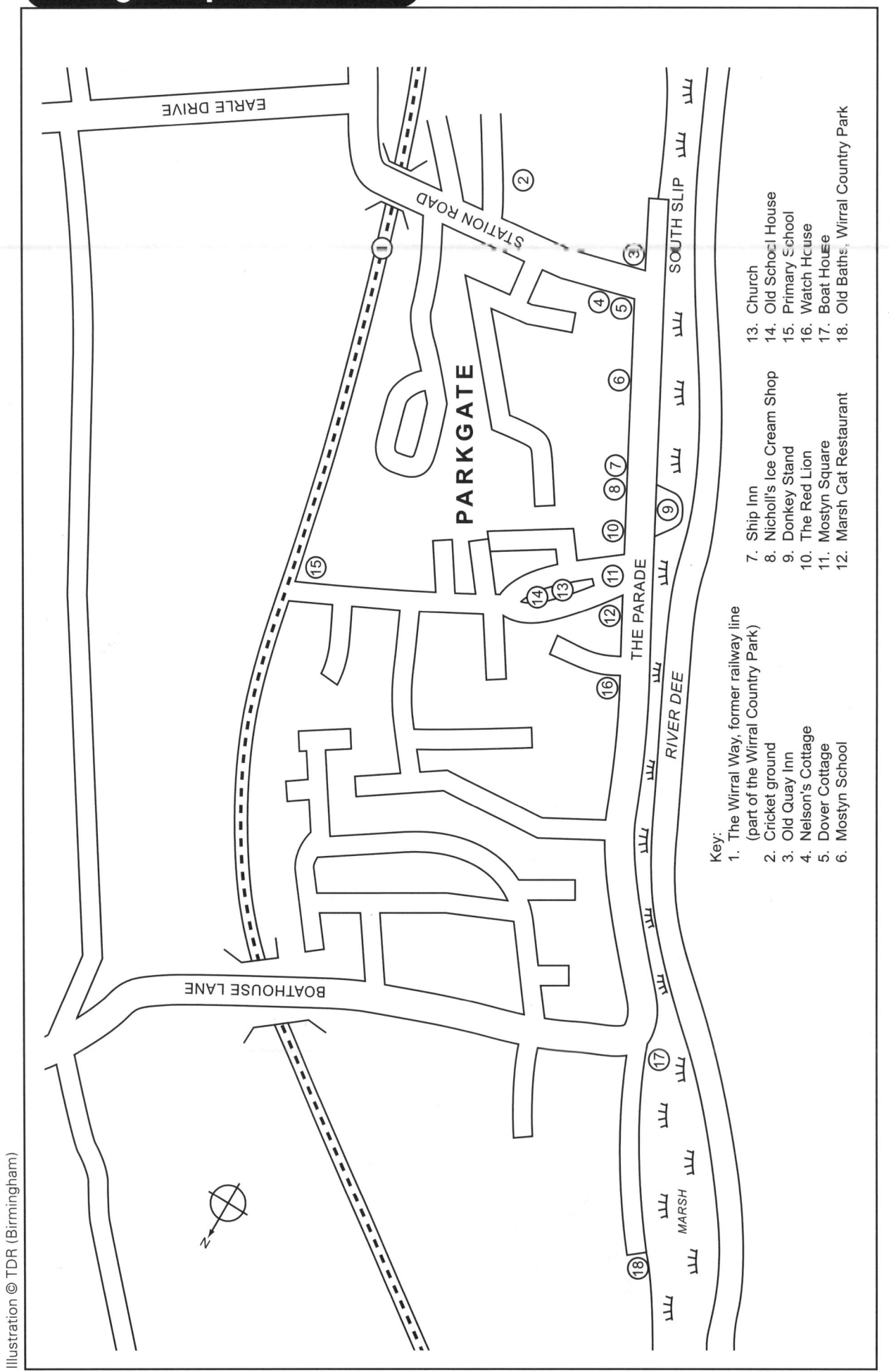

Key:
1. The Wirral Way, former railway line (part of the Wirral Country Park)
2. Cricket ground
3. Old Quay Inn
4. Nelson's Cottage
5. Dover Cottage
6. Mostyn School
7. Ship Inn
8. Nicholl's Ice Cream Shop
9. Donkey Stand
10. The Red Lion
11. Mostyn Square
12. Marsh Cat Restaurant
13. Church
14. Old School House
15. Primary School
16. Watch House
17. Boat House
18. Old Baths, Wirral Country Park

Illustration © TDR (Birmingham)